Minerals and Rocks

Chatto Nature Guides

Minerals and Rocks

Identified and Illustrated with colour photographs

Prof. Dr. Walther Schumann

Translated by Dr. Clive Bishop

English edition edited by
Dr. Alan Woolley

Chatto & Windus · London

Published by
Chatto & Windus Ltd.
40 William IV Street
London WC2N 4DF

*

Clarke, Irwin & Co Ltd
Toronto

British Library Cataloguing in Publication Data

Schumann, Walter
    Minerals and Rocks.—
        (Chatto Nature Guides)
    1. Minerology—Handbooks, manuals etc.
    2. Rocks—Identification
    I. Title   II. Woolley, Alan Robert
    549   QE363.2
ISBN 0 7011 2361 3 Hardback
ISBN 0 7011 2362 1 Paperback

© Illustrations
BLV Verlagsgesellschaft—mbh, München, 1977
English Translation © Chatto & Windus Ltd. 1978.

Printed in Italy

Introduction

It may appear presumptious to claim that it is possible to iden-
tify minerals and rocks using a small book with coloured
illustrations. There are over 2000 mineral species and many
varieties of these, and every year 30 or more new minerals are
discovered. In addition several hundreds of different kinds of
rock have been described. However, only relatively few
minerals and rocks are widely distributed or of economic importance, and it is some of these that are described and
illustrated in the following pages. The 100 minerals and 80
rocks in this book should enable some insight to be gained of
the world of minerals and rocks.

Typical representatives of minerals and rocks such as the
collector may actually find or buy, rather than rare museum
specimens, have been chosen for the coloured photographs.
At the same time they were also selected so that the reader
might be so impressed by their beauty as to be stimulated to
collect them himself.

The book is arranged in three parts. The first part (pages 6-12)
describes the arrangement of the book, and explains some
technical aspects of minerals and rocks needed to understand
the detailed descriptions. Then follow the illustrated descriptions of minerals (pages 14-111), and finally those of rocks
(pages 112-139). Meteorites and tektites are described on
pages 140-141.

It is essential to understand the difference between minerals
and rocks. The Earth is made essentially of rock, and rock is
made of the substances known as minerals. Whereas rocks are
simply mixtures of different minerals, the minerals themselves
are always the same, or nearly so. A mineral, for instance
calcite, is always made of the same chemical elements (in this
case calcium, carbon and oxygen) and in the same proportions.

Mineral names: Many minerals have more than one name; sometimes three or four. In this book the most common name is used, but the most important synonyms are also given. The names of the earliest known minerals were often miners' or local terms, but nowadays the naming of new minerals is carefully vetted by an international commission. The names often refer to outstanding qualities of the mineral, or to localities, but minerals are frequently named after people, usually mineralogists. The name nearly always ends in "ite". Gemstones are frequently given foreign sounding names of no scientific validity, probably as an incentive to purchase, and to give the impression that the stone is more valuable than in fact it is. There are codes of practice relating to names for the gemstone trade.

Gemstones: Certain minerals are prized by man for their beauty, rarity and durability. These are known as gemstones or precious stones.

Chemical composition of minerals: Each mineral described in this book is given a chemical formula. These formulae indicate the elements of which the mineral is composed, and also the relative proportions of these elements. The formula is also expressed by a 'chemical name'. The following is a list of the chemical elements, and their symbols, used in this book.

Ag	silver	Fe	iron	S	sulphur
Al	aluminium	H	hydrogen	Sb	antimony
As	arsenic	Hg	mercury	Si	silicon
Au	gold	K	potassium	Sn	tin
B	boron	Mg	magnesium	Sr	strontium
Ba	barium	Mn	manganese	Ti	titanium
Be	beryllium	Mo	molybdenum	U	uranium
C	carbon	N	nitrogen	V	vanadium
Ca	calcium	Na	sodium	W	tungsten
Cl	chlorine	Ni	nickel	Zn	zinc
Cr	chromium	O	oxygen	Zr	zirconium
Cu	copper	P	phosphorus		
F	fluorine	Pb	lead		

A mineral formula consists essentially of two parts. The first part has a positive electrical charge and is called a cation, or cationic group if it consists of more than one element. The second part has a negative electrical charge and is called an anion if of one element only, or an anionic group if of more than one element. The main anionic groups represented by the minerals described in this book and the way they are expressed verbally are as follows.

As, As_2 etc. arsenide

AsO_4 etc. arsenate

BO_3, B_3O_4 etc. borate

Cl, Cl_2 etc. chloride

CO_3 carbonate

CrO_4 chromate

F, F_2 fluoride

MoO_4 molybdate

NO_3 nitrate

O, O_2 etc. oxide

OH, $(OH)_2$ etc. hydroxide

PO_4 etc. phosphate

S, S_2 etc. sulphide

SiO_4, Si_2O_7 etc. silicate

SO_4 sulphate

WO_4 etc. tungstate

Thus $ZnCO_3$ is expressed as zinc carbonate and is the formula of the mineral smithsonite. Similarly $Be_3Al_2Si_6O_{18}$ is beryllium aluminium silicate which is the formula of the mineral beryl of which emerald is the deep green variety.

Mineral classification: Minerals can be classified in a number of different ways, but usually they are divided into classes according to their chemical composition. Organic compounds are a separate class. A chemical classification is adopted in this book, and the chemical groups with the minerals from them which are described and illustrated here are as follows.

Mineral classes	Minerals illustrated and described
i. Elements	Bismuth, copper, diamond, gold, silver, sulphur.
ii. Sulphides	Arsenopyrite, chalcosine, cinnabar, galena, marcasite, pyrite, pyrrhotine, realgar, sphalerite, stibnite.
iii. Fluorides and chlorides	Fluorite, halite.
iv. Oxides and hydroxides	Agate, amethyst, cassiterite, chalcedony, cuprite, hematite, jasper, moss agate, opal, psilomelane, quartz, rose quartz, ruby, smoky quartz, tiger's-eye, wood opal.
v. Nitrates, carbonates and borates	aragonite, azurite, calcite, cerussite, dolomite, malachite, rhodochrosite, siderite, smithsonite.
vi. Sulphates, chromates, molybdates,	Baryte, celestine, crocoite, gypsum, wulfenite.

	tungstaes	
vii.	Phosphates, arsenates, vanadates	Apatite, descloizite, mimetite, pyromorphite, turquoise, vanadinite, variscite, wavellite.
viii.	Silicates	Adularia, actinolite, almandine, amazonstone, aquamarine, benitoite, chrysocolla, chrysotile, diopside, dioptase, epidote, hemimorphite, jadeite, kunzite, kyanite, labradorite, lapis lazuli, muscovite, olivine, prehnite, rhodonite, emerald, sodalite, staurolite, topaz, tourmaline, zircon, zoisite.
ix.	Organic compounds	Amber, coral.

Mineral groups: Many minerals belong to larger groups, and these are indicated when appropriate. Thus amethyst, rose quartz, smoky quartz, tiger's eye, moss agate, chalcedony, jasper, and silicified wood are all members of the quartz group.

Physical Characteristics of Minerals

Only those physical features of minerals which are easily observed or measured are given.

Colour: Some minerals can be readily identified by their colour, but care must be taken because many minerals are variable in the colours they display. Quartz, for instance, can be almost any colour. However, used with care and experience, colour is one of the most useful characters of minerals for purposes of identification.

Streak: The colour of the powder of a mineral is much less variable than the mass colour, and can be a diagnostic feature. The easiest way to observe the powder is to draw the mineral firmly over a piece of white, unglazed tile making a mark. This is known as a 'streak'. For hard minerals such as silicates it is often difficult to obtain a streak, and if so it is of very little help.

Hardness: 150 years ago the Viennese mineralogist Friedrich Mohs proposed a ten point scale of hardness for minerals which is still used today. Each mineral in the scale will scratch those below it but will itself be scratched by those minerals higher in the scale. Minerals with the same hardness will not scratch each other.

The hardness of a mineral can be determined by scratching with other minerals of which the hardness is known, or some other material of known hardness. For instance the fingernail has a hardness of about 2½, the steel blade of a pocket knife about 5½, and minerals of hardness greater than 6 will scratch window glass.

The softest mineral on Mohs' scale is talc with a scratching hardness of 1; the hardest mineral, in fact the hardest known natural mineral, is diamond with a hardness of 10. Mohs' scale is as follows.

Mohs' hardness	Mineral	Observations
1	Talc	can be scraped with the fingernail
2	Gypsum	can be scratched with the fingernail
3	Calcite	can be scratched with a copper coin
4	Fluorite	easily scratched with a knife
5	Apatite	just scratched with a knife
6	Orthoclase	can be scratched with a steel file
7	Quartz	scratches window glass
8	Topaz	scratches quartz easily
9	Corundum	scratches topaz easily
10	Diamond	cannot be scratched.

Sets of the 10 minerals can be obtained. For the scratching test to be successful one must take care to ensure that only sharp edged pieces are used and these are drawn firmly over a clean, smooth surface of the unknown mineral. There are certain minerals in which the hardness varies from face to face and in different directions on a face.

Specific gravity: Specific gravity is the number of times heavier a substance is than an equal volume of water. Minerals with a specific gravity less than 2 feel light, those from 2 to 4 feel normal, and those greater than 4 feel heavy.

Lustre: Minerals often have a characteristic lustre. One distinguishes vitreous lustre (that of broken glass), silky lustre, pearly lustre, adamantine lustre (that of diamond), greasy and metallic lustre. Minerals that lack lustre are described as dull. The schiller effect (chatoyancy, cats-eye effect, opalescence) observed in some minerals can also be an important characteristic for recognition.

Transparency: Minerals can be transparent, translucent (that is they transmit light but only weakly), or opaque. In very thin slices most minerals are transparent or translucent. Inclusions and impurities diminish transparency.

Fracture: If a mineral is broken and the broken surface is irregular this is known as fracture. One recognizes conchoidal (the smooth, rounded, shell-like surface of broken glass), splintery, fibrous, uneven, and earthy fracture. Conchoidal fracture is typical of quartz.

Cleavage: Many minerals part along flat surfaces, a property which is known as cleavage. It results from the internal arrangement of the atoms which make the crystal. According to the ease with which the cleavage occurs one distinguishes perfect, good, and poor cleavage. The number of cleavage directions and the angles between them are also important. There are some minerals, for instance quartz, which have no cleavage.

Crystals: Minerals are made of atoms, and these are arranged in a definite and orderly way which is always the same for any particular mineral. When a mineral crystallizes freely it will form crystals bounded by flat surfaces, and the shapes of the crystals are determined by the internal arrangement of the atoms. Although there are hundreds of crystal shapes it has been discovered that they can be classified into 7 crystal systems according to their symmetry. The 7 systems are known as cubic, tetragonal, orthorhombic, monoclinic, triclinic, hexagonal and trigonal, and these are given in the descriptive sections.

There is not space here to explain how the crystal systems are defined. However, it may be noted that crystals of one system, and even crystals of the same mineral, can show considerable differences of shape. This is because a crystal is made up of crystal 'forms', which are combinations of faces determined by the symmetry of the system. There are always a number of different forms possible, but one or a number of them only may be developed. The appearance of a crystal may be described by reference to the dominant form such as cubic, octahedral, or prismatic—that is it forms prisms. The general aspect of a crystal produced by the forms it develops may also be described, and this is known as the habit. For instance, a mineral may develop flat tablets, which are described as 'tabular', or thin needles referred to as 'acicular'.

To help with this rather complicated aspect of crystals a selection of crystal shapes from all the crystal systems is shown on page 144. Also, accompanying most of the mineral descriptions there are drawings indicating some of the commonest forms adopted by those minerals.

Aggregates: Some minerals commonly form growths of a particular shape which are known as aggregates. These are often typical of a particular mineral and so can help with its identification. Minerals without regular outlines are referred to as massive. Spherical or lensoid mineral aggregates occurring within a rock are called nodules or concretions.

Other characteristics: Other features of minerals which may be helpful with identification include magnetic properties (magnetite is attracted or repelled by a magnet) and certain optical properties. Such characteristics are referred to in the descriptive section when appropriate.

Occurrence: Some minerals are of widespread occurrence, whereas others are restricted to particular geological environments. This, together with the nature of the minerals usually found accompanying a particular mineral, is often very helpful with identification.

Locality: Only a few localities are mentioned, being selected because they produce, or did produce, particularly fine specimens, or because they are of economic significance, or because they are historically famous.

Uses: Many minerals are needed as raw materials in industry, for use as jewellery, or serve as the raw material of the collector or lapidary.

Rocks

Rocks are divided into three groups, according to how they were formed, namely 'igneous', 'sedimentary' and 'metamorphic' rocks.

Igneous rocks were originally molten, being formed from liquid rock material, known as magma, which originates deep down in the Earth. They can be divided into 'plutonic' igneous rocks, which are those in which the magma crystallised within the Earth as 'intrusions', and 'volcanic' or 'extrusive' igneous rocks in which the molten magma crystallised at or on the Earth's surface. Generally plutonic rocks are coarse-grained because they cooled slowly at depth allowing the minerals to grow, whereas volcanic rocks are chilled quickly and so tend to be fine-grained.

Sedimentary rocks are formed at the Earth's surface. They are produced from the soft sediment, such as sand and mud, which is being produced all the time by the weathering and breakdown of other rocks. The sediment accumulates, principally in the sea, and with time hardens into sedimentary rocks such as sandstone and mudstone. Sedimentary rocks often contain fossils.

Metamorphic rocks are formed deep within the Earth. If igneous or sedimentary rocks are buried deeply they are subjected to high pressures and high, often very high, temperatures. This causes the rock to acquire a new aspect, principally because the minerals recrystallise and grow, and new minerals develop.

Texture: The texture of rocks is determined by the relationship of the individual mineral grains. In igneous rocks the grains tend to be closely interlocking and, according to their size, may be coarse, medium, or fine-grained. All the grains may be about the same size, or some crystals may be much larger than others when the rock is said to be porphyritic.

Sedimentary rocks, being formed from the breakdown of preexisting rocks, are often made of recognisable grains or fragments, though this is not always the case. Metamorphic rocks are very variable in texture, depending on the nature of the original material and the intensity of the metamorphism. Many metamorphic rocks, however, are rich in platy minerals, such as micas, which tend to lie in a parallel or foliated attitude which gives the rock a distinctive layered aspect described as 'schistosity', the rock being referred to as a 'schist'.

Structure and field relationships: Among the larger features of rocks which are useful for purposes of recognition are the structures they display. Sedimentary rocks, for instance, are typically layered or bedded. This bedding reflects the accumulation of sediment, probably on the bottom of the sea, layer by layer. Metamorphic rocks are also commonly layered and whilst this may be inherited from the bedding of original sedimentary rocks which have been metamorphosed, it is frequently due to recrystallisation during the metamorphic processes.

The overall disposition of rocks on a large scale, known as their 'field relationships', is perhaps the best way of recognising igneous rocks, particularly the intrusive ones. Plutonic igneous rocks, for instance, were intruded into other rocks in a molten state, and so can be seen to cut sharply across them. Also being hot they bake or metamorphose the rocks with which they are in contact, and this is one of the ways in which metamorphic rocks are produced.

Mineral composition: The main minerals of which most rocks are composed are known as the essential or rock-forming minerals, while those that occur in small amounts are called accessory minerals. The rock-forming minerals are only a few in number—perhaps no more than a dozen constitute all the commoner rocks, although most of these minerals are complex and variable in composition.

Many minerals are restricted to either igneous, sedimentary, or metamorphic rocks, and a knowledge of those rock types to which particular minerals are restricted is obviously very useful for the mineral collector.

Rock names: Rocks are named firstly according to their origin, that is igneous, sedimentary or metamorphic, then according to the mineralogy, and sometimes to the texture or structures. For instance granite is a plutonic igneous rock of feldspar (of a particular type) with at least 20 per cent of quartz. If it contains biotite mica and has some feldspars much larger than the others then it would be called a 'porphyritic biotite granite'. A strongly foliated metamorphic rock of biotite mica and garnet would be called a garnet-biotite schist. By this means the rock name, if properly used, can give a considerable amount of information about the rock being described.

For Illustrations of the crystal systems see page 144

Copper

Cu   Native copper

Characteristics: Colour copper-red, tarnishes brown, green patina. Streak shining, metallic copper-red, (metallic shine). Hardness 2½-3. Spec. Gravity 8.5-9.0. Metallic lustre, opaque, translucent in very thin sheets. fracture hackly, very malleable and ductile. No cleavage. Crystals (cubic system) rarely regularly developed (cubic or rhombdodecahedral), mostly strongly distorted, aggregates finely branching, also as crusts.—**Occurrence:** Oxidised zones of copper ore deposits, associated with apophylite, calcite, chlorite, cuprite, malachite, chalcosine, prehnite, zeolites.—**Localities:** East and West Germany (Mansfeld; Zwickau); Austria (Mitterberg, Salzburg); Rumania (Banak); Sweden (Falun); USA (Bingham, Utah, Arizona; Montana; Michigan); Zaire (Katanga); USSR (Urals; Turan). The world's resources of copper could be exhausted in a few decades.—**Uses:** Electrical industry (very good conductor of electricity), construction of machinery, radio industry, printing (copper plate engraving). Because it forms a corrosion resistant green patina on exposure to air, copper is used for roofs, gutters and coins. Copper compounds are widely used in insecticides and fungicides. Copper was worked in Cyprus and the Sinai peninsula about 4000 B.C. Bronze (an alloy of 70-90% copper and 30-5% tin) was, by reason of its great toughness, the most important material used in the Bronze Age period for weapons and tools. Today bronze is used for sculpture and for bells. Other copper alloys are brass (up to 70% copper with zinc) and the corrosion resistant nickel silver (German silver) (45-70% copper, 8-28% nickel and 8-45% tin).—**Illustration:** Native copper from Santa Rita, Mexico.

Bismuth

Bi   Native bismuth

Characteristics: Colour silver-white becoming reddish when tarnished. Streak, silver-white. Hardness 2-2½. Spec. Gravity 9.7-9.8. Metallic lustre, opaque. Fracture, fine-grained, brittle. Cleavage, perfect. Crystals (trigonal system) very rare and indistinct rhombohedra which resemble cubes, aggregates feathery branching, dendritic, foliated, compact, granular.—**Occurrence:** Veins, occasionally also as nuggets in alluvial deposits. Accompanied by nickel, cobalt, uranium, silver, lead and zinc minerals.—**Localities:** Cornwall and Devon; France (Meymac; Corrèze); Spain (Pozoblanco); Bolivia; Australia (Queensland; New South Wales).—**Uses:** Important ore of bismuth. Bismuth is necessary for the manufacture of bearings, easily melted alloys for printing type, and also in radiography.—**Illustration:** Dendritic bismuth from Mackenheim, Odenwald, Germany.

Diamond

C   Carbon

Characteristics: Colour yellow, brown, colourless, occasionally green, blue, reddish, black. Streak white. Hardness 10. Spec. Gravity 3.5-3.6. Adamantine lustre, transparent to opaque. Fracture conchoidal. Cleavage perfect. Crystals (cubic system) predominantly octahedra, also cubes, rhombdodecahedra. Twins. Finely granular material is called bort.—**Occurrence:** In kimberlite pipes and alluvial deposits. Synthetic diamonds have been available since 1955 and are used exclusively in industry.—**Localities:** Zaire; USSR; South Africa; Ghana; South West Africa and in many other countries, principally in Africa and South America.—**Uses:** Clear quality (about 20% of total production) for jewellery, others, by reason of their great hardness, for cutting, grinding and polishing.—**Illustration:** left, diamond aggregate. Centre, diamond octahedron in kimberlite. Right, crystal group, South Africa (⅔ natural size).

Gold

Au   Native gold

Characteristics: Colour golden yellow to brassy yellow. Streak golden yellow. Hardness 2½-3. Spec. Gravity 15.5-19.3. Metallic lustre, opaque, translucent in thin sheets. Fracture hackly, malleable, very ductile. No cleavage. Crystals (cubic system) seldom well formed, mostly strongly distorted. Aggregates wiry and mossy, feathery, arborescent, platy, nodular (nuggets).—**Occurrence:** Native in veins, and alluvial gold in river deposits.—**Localities:** Worldwide, if only in small amounts; presently in Rumania (Siebenbürgen); N. Sweden (Boliden); Yugoslavia (Serbia); France (Massif Central); South Africa (Transvaal); Ghana; USSR (Urals, Siberia); Alaska; Canada (Ontario; British Columbia); Brazil (Minas Gerais); Western Australia.—**Uses:** Jewellery, monetary standard, medicinal purposes.—**Illustration:** Gold on quartz, California, U.S.A.

Silver

Ag   Native silver

Characteristics: Colour silver-white, tarnishes to black. Streak silver-white. Hardness 2½-3. Spec. Gravity 9.6-11.0. Metallic lustre, opaque. Fracture hackly, ductile, malleable. No cleavage. Crystals (cubic system) cubic and octahedral, but very rare and mostly distorted. Aggregates predominantly compact, wiry and hairlike, dendritic and feathery, also as plates, grains and nodules.—**Occurrence:** In pockets or disseminated in silver ores. frequently mixed with gold.—**Localities:** Saxony (Freiberg); Czechoslovakia (Joachimsthal); Norway (Kongsberg); Canada (Cobalt); USA (Nevada); Mexico; Bolivia.—**Uses:** Pure silver in photographic industry. Alloyed with copper for manufacture of silverware. The silver-bearing minerals argentite (silver glance), freibergite and ruby silvers (pyrargyrite and proustite) are more important ores of silver than is native silver.—**Illustration:** Hairlike native silver from Kongsberg, Norway. (Width of the original 6cm).

Pyrite   Iron Pyrites
FeS₂   *Iron sulphide*

Characteristics: Colour light brassy yellow. Streak greenish black. Hardness 6-6½. Spec. gravity 4.9-5.2. Metallic lustre. Fracture conchoidal to uneven. Cleavage imperfect. Crystals (cubic system) usually cubes, also pyritohedra and other forms. Cube faces commonly striated parallel to edges. Frequently twinned. Aggregates radial, reniform, bulbous, compact, granular. Most of the so-called marcasite nodules are of pyrite aggregates.—**Occurrence:** Constituent mineral of igneous rocks. veins, concretions in sedimentary rocks, occasionally in lignite and coal.—**Localities:** A widely distributed mineral, the most common sulphide. Fine material has come from many localities in Cornwall, and from Devon; also Italy (Piemont; Elba); Norway (Grong); Sweden (Falun); Spain (Huelva); Portugal (Alemtejo).—**Uses:** Manufacture of sulphuric acid; an important source of sulphur.—**Illustration:** Pyrite group from Elba, Italy.

Sulphur
S   Native sulphur

Characteristics: Colour yellow, brownish when impure. Streak white. Hardness 1½-2. Spec. Gravity 2.0-2.1. Adamantine lustre on crystal faces, resinous lustre on fractured surfaces, transparent to translucent. Fracture conchoidal, uneven. Cleavage none. Crystals (orthorhombic system) bipyramidal, tabular. Aggregates compact, coarse-grained to dense, earthy, crusty, powdery as coatings.—**Occurrence:** Volcanic sublimation product or in sedimentary rocks, where it results from the decomposition of sulphur compounds or gypsum-bearing sediments, in beds and veins. Associated minerals are aragonite, calcite, celestine, gypsum, halite.—**Localities:** Sicily (Agrigento); Poland (Upper Silesia); USA (Louisiana; Texas); Mexico; Chile; USSR (Middle Volga area); Japan; Indonesia.—**Uses:** For manufacture of sulphuric acid; insecticides and fungicides, rubber and paper industries, matches, fireworks and as a colouring agent.—**Illustration:** Group of sulphur crystals from Mexico (⅔ natural size).

Stibnite Antimonite

Sb₂S₃ Antimony Sulphide

Characteristics: Colour lead-grey, dull, black or with coloured tarnish. Streak lead-grey. Hardness 2. Spec. Gravity 4.5-4.6. Metallic lustre, opaque. Fracture subconchoidal. One perfect cleavage parallel to length of crystals. Crystals (orthorhombic system), long prismatic, with striations parallel to their length; sometimes kinked into wavy forms, bent and twisted about their long axis, deeply furrowed along their length. Aggregates radiating, dense, rarely granular or felted.—**Occurrence:** In veins of quartz, lead ore and silver ore, often together with native gold. Less commonly also with deposits of orpiment, realgar, and cinnabar. Other associated minerals are baryte, calcite, fluorite and kaolinite.—**Localities:** Germany (Wolfsberg, Westphalia); Yugoslavia (Lesnica); France (Auvergne); Czechoslovakia (Bohemia; Slovakia); Algeria (Jebel Haminate near Constantine); Bolivia; Mexico; Japan (Shikoku); China (Hunan Province); Western Australia (Wiluna).—**Uses:** Most important ore of antimony. Antimony is used for making alloys with lead and tin (imparting hardness for bearings and type metal), in the rubber industry, in the textile industry, for safety matches, for burnishing gun barrels and also in medicine. Formerly antimony was used as eyeshadow. In the Middle Ages alchemists used it for the purification of gold.—**Illustration:** Acicular stibnite group from Pribram, Czechoslovakia.

Marcasite

FeS₂   Iron Sulphide

Characteristics: Colour brassy yellow, sometimes with a coloured tarnish. Streak greyish-black. Hardness 6-6½. Spec. Gravity 4.8-4.9. Metallic lustre, opaque. Fracture uneven. Cleavage poor. Crystals (orthorhombic system) tabular, short columnar. Aggregates radiating fibres; may have cockscomb form or, when twinned, be spear-shaped. Compact aggregates difficult to distinguish from pyrite. Most of the so-called marcasite nodules are in fact pyrite.—**Occurrence:** In veins, cavities, concretions in sedimentary rocks. Rarely forms large deposits. Associated minerals are pyrite, sphalerite, wurtzite, chalcopyrite, quartz.—**Localities:** In the chalk of Kent, between Folkestone and Dover, also around Tavistock, Devon, and Weardale, Durham. Also USSR (Urals); USA (Missouri); Bolivia.—**Uses:** Manufacture of sulphuric acid.—**Illustration:** Marcasite group from Vinitrov, Bohemia, Czechoslovakia.

Cinnabar

HgS   Mercury Sulphide

Characteristics: Colour red to brownish, occasionally grey. Streak red. Hardness 2-2½. Spec. Gravity 8.0-8.2. Adamantine lustre, opaque, transparent in very thin slices. Fracture uneven. Cleavage perfect. Crystals (trigonal system) thick tabular, rhombohedral or cube-like, but rare and small. Interpenetration twins characteristic.—**Occurrence:** Veins, impregnations. In spite of low hardness occasionally also found in alluvial deposits.—**Localities:** Spain (Almaden); Italy (Serravezza, Tuscany); Yugoslavia (Mt. Avala); USSR (Donetz basin); USA (Texas; California); China (Hunan Province).—**Uses:** Most important ore of mercury, which is used mainly in the armaments industry (percussion caps) and as an amalgam with gold and silver; also in thermometers.—**Illustration:** Cinnabar crystals (reddish) on matrix, Almaden, Spain.

Chalcopyrite

CuFeS₂   Copper iron sulphide

Characteristics: Colour brassy yellow to golden yellow, often with a multi-coloured tarnish; may also tarnish black. Streak greenish-black. Hardness 3½-4 (most important feature distinguishing it from pyrite which has a similar appearance). Spec. Gravity 4.1-4.3 Metallic lustre, opaque. Fracture conchoidal. Cleavage very poor. Crystals (tetragonal system) appear tetrahedral, rare, mostly small, often distorted, frequently twinned. Aggregates compact, disseminated. Weathers to yield malachite, azurite and chrysocolla.—**Occurrence:** Good crystals only in cavities, in Veins, small amounts occasionally in coal. Associated minerals are galena, pyrrhotine, pyrite, sphalerite.—**Localities:** Devon and Cornwall; Isle of Man; Sweden (Falun); Spain (Rio Tinto); USSR (Urals); and many other localities.—**Uses:** Important copper ore.—**Illustration:** Chalcopyrite crystal group with siderite, Herdorf, Siegerland, Germany.

Galena

PbS   Lead sulphide

Characteristics: Colour lead-grey, streak lead-grey. Hardness 2½. Spec. Gravity 7.4-7.6. Bright metallic lustre, dull tarnish, opaque. Fracture subchoncoidal or even; brittle. Cleavage perfect parallel to cube faces. Crystals (cubic system) mostly distinct cubes, octahedra, twins. Faces may be partially flawed and bent. Large crystals known. Aggregates compact coarse to fine-grained. Frequently in close association with sphalerite, pyrite, and chalcopyrite.—**Occurrence:** In ore veins with sphalerite and in sedimentary rocks as beds or impregnations.—**Localities:** Widely distributed: Numerous localities in Cornwall; also North Wales; Weardale, Durham; Cumbria; and Southern Scotland; also Czechoslovakia (Pribram); Yugoslavia (Trepca); Spain (Almeria); Sweden (Sala); USA (Missouri; Leadville, Colorado); Australia (Broken Hill, New South Wales).—**Uses:** Most important and commonest ore of lead. Worked as long ago as 3000 B.C. Lead is used as a radiation shield.—**Illustration:** Galena group with some calcite, Siegen, Westphalia, Germany.

Realgar

AsS   Arsenic sulphide

Characteristics: Colour orange-red, rarely dark red. Streak orange-red. Hardness 1½-2. Spec. Gravity 3.5. Lustre resinous. Transparent to translucent. Fracture conchoidal, splintery. Cleavage good. Crystals (monoclinic system) mainly small and short prismatic with striations parallel to their length. On exposure to light realgar alters to earthy or powdery orpiment. Aggregates compact, coarse to fine-grained, also as coatings.—**Occurrence:** Deposited from hot waters. Sublimation product of volcanoes, in limestone, dolomite and argillaceous rocks. Associated minerals are stibnite, arsenic, orpiment, baryte, calcite, pyrite, sphalerite.—**Localities:** Switzerland (Binnental); Czechoslovakia (Erzgebirge); Rumania (Siebenbürgen); Italy (Vesuvius); Yugoslavia (Bosnia): USA (Utah; Nevada).—**Uses:** Raw material for the production of arsenic. Compounds are used in the glass industry, and for paints and fireworks.—**Illustration:** Realgar crystals on limestone, King County, Washington, USA.

Arsenopyrite   Mispickel

FeAsS   Iron arsenic sulphide

Characteristics: Colour of crystal faces is tin-white, of fractured surfaces steel-grey, frequently tarnished brownish. Streak greyish-black. Hardness 5½-6. Spec. gravity 5.9-6.2. Bright metallic lustre, opaque. Fracture uneven, brittle. Cleavage indistinct. Crystals (monoclinic system) predominantly columnar which rhombic in section, some faces coarsely striated, frequently twinned. Crystals distinct or intergrown. Aggregates compact, granular to dense, elongated, finely fibrous, also disseminated.—**Occurrence:** In veins mostly associated with other ore minerals. Such as those of tungsten, tin, and silver.—**Localities:** Numerous localities in Devon and Cornwall, also Austria (Mitterberg, Salzburg); Sweden (Boliden); USA (California); USSR (Urals; Eastern Siberia).—**Uses:** Production of arsenic. Arsenopyrite is the most important ore of arsenic.—**Illustration:** Arsenopyrite group with calcite crystals, Trepca, Yugoslavia.

Sphalerite   Blende

Zinc Blende
ZnS   Zinc sulphide

Characteristics: Colour yellow, red, brown, greenish, black, rarely colourless. Streak yellowish to light brown. Hardness 3½-4. Spec. Gravity 3.9-4.1. Lustre resinous, almost metallic lustre in opaque specimens, also bright vitreous lustre, transparent to opaque. Fracture conchoidal, brittle. Cleavage perfect. Crystals (cubic system) strongly distorted and ridged. Develops tetrahedra, rhombdodecahedra and cubes, often in combination. Nearly always forms twins with facial striations. Aggregates fine to coarse-grained.—**Occurrence:** Many different kinds of deposit; e.g., in veins in limestone and dolomite. Associated minerals are baryte, galena, calcite, fluorite, chalcosine, marcasite, pyrite, quartz, wurtzite.—**Localities:** Alston Moor, Cumbria; Weardale, Durham; many places in Cornwall; Wanlockhead, Dumfries; Isle of Man; also Sweden (Ammeberg); Switzerland (Binnental); USSR (Eastern Siberia); USA (Idaho; Kansas; Missouri; New Jersey; Oklahoma); Mexico (Chivera).—**Uses:** Most important ore of zinc, the main producer of which is the USA, followed by Mexico, Australia, West Germany and Poland. Zinc is used for galvanising iron to prevent corrosion, for the production of brass (alloy of copper and tin) and for batteries. The various compounds of zinc have a further wide range of uses. Beautifully coloured sphalerite is cut as a gemstone by collectors.—**Illustration:** Group of black sphalerite crystals with typical twin-striations encrusting delicate pink rhodochrosite and white calcite, Trepca, Yugoslavia.

Pyrrhotine

FeS   Iron sulphide

Characteristics: Colour bronze yellow with a brownish tinge. Streak grey-black. Hardness 3½-4½. Spec. Gravity 4.6-4.7. Metallic lustre, dull tarnish, opaque. Fracture subconchoidal uneven, brittle. crystals part parallel to the base; occasionally magnetic. Crystals (hexagonal system) rare, hexagonal plates, short prisms, rose-like groups. aggregates compact, granular to dense.—**Occurrence:** In igneous rocks such as gabbro, more rarely in pegmatites or metamorphic rocks, also in sedimentary rocks. Associated minerals are arsenopyrite, galena, cassiterite, ilmenite, chalcopyrite, magnetite, pentlandite, pyrite, siderite, and sphalerite.—**Localities:** Kirkcudbrightshire, and in some of the old mines of Cornwall; Finland; Norway (Kongsberg); Yugoslavia (Trepca); Italy (Bottino, Tuscany).—**Uses:** Used sometimes in the production of sulphuric acid.—**Illustration:** Pyrrhotine aggregate with siderite, Trepca, Yugoslavia.

Halite   Rock salt

NaCl   Sodium chloride

Characteristics: Colour white, grey, yellow, blue, red, colourless. Streak white. Hardness 2½. Spec. Gravity 2.1-2.2. Vitreous lustre, greasy lustre on weathering. Fracture conchoidal, brittle. Cleavage perfect. Soluble in water at room temperature. Taste salty (though, for obvious reasons, minerals should not normally be tasted). Strongly hygroscopic, that is, it attracts moisture from the atmosphere and becomes wet. Crystals (cubic system) predominantly cubes, often distorted. Aggregates compact, granular, fibrous, stalactitic.—**Occurrence:** Normally as layers, often very thick, in sedimentary rocks; saltdomes (these are upward bulges of rock salt which may penetrate the overlying rocks).—**Localities:** Mined at Nantwich, Cheshire; also at Carrickfergus, Country Antrim and in Austria (Salzburg); Poland (Cracow); Spain (Barcelona Province); and many other places.—**Uses:** For seasoning and preserving food, as salt lick for animals, in large amounts in industry (chemical industry, soap manufacture, medicine).—**Illustration:** Group of cubes from Heringen, Germany.

Fluorite   Fluorspar   *CaF₂*   *Calcium fluoride*

Characteristics: Colour violet, blue, black, yellow, green, rarely colourless, occasionally core and rim differently coloured. Streak white. Hardness 4. Spec. Gravity 3.2. Vitreous lustre, transparent, opaque when very strongly coloured. Fracture subconchoidal. Cleavage perfect parallel to octahedral faces. Crystals (cubic system) frequently well formed, predominantly cubes and octahedra, also combinations of these forms. frequently twinned. Cube faces are occasionally striated parallel to edges. Aggregates compact, granular, sometimes banded, fluorescent (the phenomenon of fluorescence is named after this mineral).—**Occurrence:** In igneous and sedimentary rocks, but particularly in veins. —**Localities:** Many places in England including Northumberland, Durham, Cumbria, Derbyshire and Cornwall. Bavaria (Wolsendorf).—**Uses:** As a flux in the smelting of iron to lower the temperature of smelting. In the manufacture of glass and ceramics and in the optical industry; also for the manufacture of hydrofluoric acid.—**Illustration:** Fluorite group from Mexico (4/5 natural size).

Ruby   (Corundum group)   *Al₂O₃*   *Aluminium oxide*

Characteristics: Colour red. Streak white. Hardness 9. Spec. Gravity 3.9-4.1. Vitreous lustre, adamantine lustre when cut and polished, opaque to transparent. fracture conchoidal, uneven. No cleavage. Crystals (trigonal system) usually barrel-shaped, prismatic, columnar, also flat tabular. Aggregates compact, intergrown, fine and coarse-grained masses. The correct name for the mineral having the chemical composition Al₂O₃ is 'Corundum'. The name ruby is given to deep red varieties, and sapphire to blue varieties.—**Occurrence:** In pegmatites and metamorphic rocks, rarely in basalt. Also found in sands and gravels, usually deposited by rivers. Synthetic ruby has been manufactured since the beginning of this century.—**Localities:** Gem quality ruby in Burma (Mogok); Thailand (Chantabun); Sri Lanka (Ratnapura); and Tanzania; poorer stones from Norway, Switzerland (Ticino); Turkey (Izmir); USSR (Urals, Kazakhstan); USA (North Carolina); Canada (Ontario).—**Uses:** Transparent gem quality ruby for jewellery, others as grinding and polishing material (e.g., emery), and used as bearings for watches and instruments.—**Illustration:** Ruby in quartz, Norway. Cut ruby 1.14 carats, Burma.

Cuprite

Cu₂O   Copper oxide

Characteristics: Colour brown-red, carmine, lead-grey. Streak brown-red. Hardness 3½-4. Spec. Gravity 5.8-6.1. Sub metallic to adamantine lustre, opaque to translucent. Fracture uneven. Cleavage none. Crystals (cubic system) octahedra, rarely cubes and rhombdodecahedra. Aggregates massive, granular. Often associated with native copper.—**Occurrence:** In copper ore deposits as a result of the alteration of other copper minerals. Associated minerals are native copper, azurite, and malachite.—**Localities:** From a number of localities in Cornwall including the Liskeard, Redruth and Truro areas; also France (Chessy, near Lyon); Spain; USSR (Urals; Altai); USA (Arizona); South West Africa (Tsumeb); Peru; and Chile.—**Uses:** Important ore of copper. Carmine-red cuprite is, in spite of its low hardness, facetted by collectors.—**Illustration:** Cuprite crystals on matrix, South West Africa.

Hematite

Fe₂O₃   Iron oxide

Characteristics: Colour black, grey-black, brown-red. Streak red. Hardness 5-6. Spec. Gravity 4.9-5.3. Metallic lustre, opaque. Fracture uneven. No cleavage. Crystals (trigonal system) distinct or intergrown, rhombohedral or tabular. Varieties with distinct crystal form are called specular iron ore or iron glance. Aggregates compact, granular, fibrous, scaly, radiating forms with a hemispherical mamillated appearance known as kidney iron ore.—**Occurrence:** In bedded masses and veins, dense aggregates, also forms rocks in which it occurs as tiny spheres usually about 1mm across known as ooliths.—**Localities:** Fine mamillated specimens have come from Cleator Moor, Cumbria; also from Sweden (Gellivara); Italy (Elba); Rumania (Banat); USSR (Ekaterinburg, Urals); USA (Lake Superior region, and elsewhere).—**Uses:** Important ore of iron. Dense varieties facetted or polished for jewellery.—**Illustration:** Fine group of crystals, Elba, Italy.

Psilomelane

No fixed chemical composition
A mixture of manganese oxides.

Characteristics: Colour black to dark grey. Streak black-brown or black. Hardness 5-7 in compact varieties. Spec. Gravity 3.3-4.7. Submetallic lustre when compact, dull in loose varieties, opaque. Fracture conchoidal, brittle. No cleavage. Usually massive in rounded or stalactitic masses.—**Occurrence:** In sedimentary rocks. Associated minerals are beryl, calcite, limonite, polianite, pyrolusite, siderite.—**Localities:** In Cornwall at Lanlivery; USSR; Ghana; South Africa; India.—**Uses:** Psilomelane is an important ore of manganese which is commonly added to iron and steel and used in the production of corrosion resistant alloys.—**Illustration:** A mass of psilomelane showing mamillated (rounded) and stalactitic forms. The radiating internal structure can be seen where broken, Westerwald, Hessen, Germany.

Cassiterite

SnO_2 Tin oxide

Characteristics: Colour black, brown, yellowish. Streak white to greyish. Hardness 6-7. Spec. gravity 6.8-7.1. Adamantine to submetallic lustre, transparent to opaque. fracture uneven. Cleavage imperfect. Crystals (tetragonal system) short prismatic or pyramidal, frequently twinned. Aggregates compact, granular to dense, also fibrous when called wood tin.—**Occurrence:** In pegmatites, veins and impregnations. Frequently in rolled grains as so called stream tin. Associated minerals are galena, chalcosine, muscovite, orthoclase, pyrite, quartz, stannite, sphalerite.—**Localities:** Numerous localities in Cornwall,where it often occurs as very fine crystals, also as wood and stream tin; Bolivia; Malaysia; Indonesia; South West Africa.—**Uses:** Most important ore of tin. Stones of light, matching colours are cut by collectors for jewellery.—**Illustration:** Cassiterite crystals on matrix, Ehrenfriedersdorf, Saxony, Germany.

Rock Crystal (Quartz group)

SiO₂ Silicon oxide

Characteristics: Colourless. Streak white. Hardness 7. Spec. Gravity 2.65. Vitreous lustre, transparent. Fracture conchoidal, brittle. No cleavage. Crystals (trigonal system) mainly six-sided prisms terminated by six faces. Prism faces with cross striations. While most crystals are found on matrix, there are also doubly terminated well shaped forms. Giant crystals a metre or more long are known Twinning common but only rarely observed in crystals. Occasional inclusions of asbestos, chlorite, goethite, gold, hornblonde, pyrite, tourmaline. Until the 17th century the word crystal was synonymous with crystalline quartz, but with the development of the science of crystallography, all minerals with plane bounding surfaces became known as crystals, and the ancient name rock-crystal was retained for the clear variety of quartz.—**Occurrence:** By reason of its resistance to mechanical and chemical attack at the earth's surface quartz is widely distributed in sedimentary rocks. Quartz is the principal constituent of most sandstones and all quartzites. Beautifully developed crystals usually occur in joints and in cavities.—**Localities:** Fine crystals come from Cumbria and Cornwall. Large crystalline forms in joints in the Alps; USSR (Urals); Brazil; Madagascar, and other localities.—**Uses:** Important raw material for the glass and ceramic industries, in technology by reason of its piezoelectrical effects it has been used for a considerable time for the generation of ultrasonics and for the modulation of transmitters and watches; nowadays, synthetic crystals, are used for these purposes. Since ancient times colourless and transparent quartz crystals and those containing decorative inclusions have been fashioned mainly into objets d'art, and also worked into jewellery. Completely clear stones have served as imitation diamonds and have gone under such names as 'Bristol diamonds'.—**Illustration:** Rock crystal group from Brazil.

Amethyst (Quartz group)

SiO₂   Silicon oxide

Characteristics: Colour pale to deep violet, sometimes strongest at the tips of the crystals. Streak white. Hardness 7. Spec. Gravity 2.65. Vitreous lustre, transparent. Fracture conchoidal, brittle. No cleavage. Crystals (trigonal system) the same as for rock crystal. Aggregates in the form of crystal groups in cavities, also compact, frequently enclosed, banded and striped with milky quartz.—**Occurrence:** In cavities, on joints and in alluvial deposits.—**Localities:** Austria (Tyrol); Brazil; Uruguay; Madagascar.—**Uses:** Best examples are used for semi-precious stones and also for objets d'art. Weakly coloured stones are heated to about 500°C when they take on a yellow or reddish brown colour similar to that of citrine and topaz. Many misleading trade names are used for such varieties.—**Illustration:** Part of an amethyst-lined cavity, Brazil.

Smoky Quartz (Quartz group)

SiO₂   Silicon oxide

Characteristics: Colour brown to black, smoky grey. Very dark varieties are known commercially as morion. Streak white. Hardness 7. Spec. Gravity 2.65. Vitreous lustre, transparent to translucent. Fracture conchoidal, brittle. No cleavage. Crystals (trigonal system) as for rock crystal. Aggregates as crystal groups, also compact, occasionally with needly inclusions of rutile.—**Occurrence:** In cavities, veins, rarely in alluvial deposits.—**Localities:** A variety known as cairngorm is common in Scotland; and found in the Cairngorm Mountains, also in the Alps; Urals; Brazil; Madagascar.—**Uses:** Transparent quality as gemstone or for objets d'art. Smoky quartz with inclusions much coveted. Poorer varieties, when heated to temperatures of about 300-400°C, take on a yellow, brown or reddish brown colour.—**Illustration:** Smoky quartz with six-rayed inclusions of rutile on a core of hematite, Brazil.

Tiger's-eye (Quartz group)

SiO₂ Silicon oxide

Characteristics: Colour golden yellow. By reason of its fibrous structure a polished or facetted cabochon has a narrow gleaming light like the eye of a tiger. Hardness 7. Spec. Gravity 2.6-2.7. Silky lustre on broken and polished surfaces-opaque. Fracture fibrous. No cleavage. Crystals (trigonal system) unknown, only fibrous parallel aggregates.—**Occurrence:** Joint filling in quartz-rich rocks, in which the fibres of the tiger's-eye are perpendicular to the joint surfaces. Tiger's-eye is formed by the replacement of crocidolite (a type of hornblende) by quartz.—**Localities:** South West Africa; Western Australia; Burma; India; USA (California).—**Uses:** for fashionable jewellery and objets d'art.—**Illustration:** Cut tiger's-eye, Griqualand, South West Africa.

Rose Quartz (Quartz group)

SiO₂ Silicon oxide

Characteristics: Colour rose pink, also pale violet, mainly somewhat dull, the colour may become paler on exposure to light. Streak white. Hardness 7. Spec. Gravity 2.65. Vitreous lustre, transparent to translucent. fracture conchoidal, brittle. No cleavage. Crystals (trigonal system) very rare, clear crystals first discovered in Brazil in 1959; mainly hexagonal prisms with 'pyramidal' end faces. Aggregates compact, usually strongly cracked.—**Occurrence:** In cavities and in pegmatite veins.—**Localities:** Japan (Yoshima); Burma (Mogok); Finland; Brazil (Minas Gerais, Bahia); Madagascar; U.S.A. (Maine; Colorado; California; South Dakota); USSR (Urals); South West Africa.—**Uses:** Strongly coloured specimens for jewellery as cabachons and necklaces, also cut for use as objets d'art; transparent stones also suitable for facetting.—**Illustration:** Rose quartz crystals, Minas Gerais, Brazil.

Moss Agate (Quartz group)

SiO_2 Silicon oxide with small amount of manganese

Characteristics: Colour white to colourless with green inclusions. Streak white. Hardness about 6½. Spec. Gravity about 2.6. Waxy to vitreous lustre, translucent. Fracture conchoidal. No cleavage. Moss agate is an aggregate formed from translucent chalcedony and inclusions of manganese oxide, which give to the stone an appearance of moss. It is actually neither true agate, nor are they true plant impressions. When densely filled with inclusions it is known commercially as moss jasper. By oxidation it acquires brown and red colours so that moss agate can appear spotted.—**Occurrence:** Cleavage filling, pebbles.—**Localities:** India; China; USA (Colorado; Michigan).—**Uses:** Cut into thin slices, so that the mossy markings are clearly seen, and then mounted as rings, pendants and other objects.—**Illustration:** Cut moss agate, India.

Chalcedony (Quartz group)

SiO_2 Silicon oxide

Characteristics: Colour white-grey, bluish. Streak white. Hardness about 6½. Spec. Gravity about 2.6 Waxy to vitreous lustre, translucent to opaque. Fracture conchoidal. No cleavage. Aggregates fibrous, radiating, stalactitic, botryoidal or reniform. Somewhat porous—variously coloured varieties are given special names: carnelian (red to reddish-brown) sard (light to dark brown-red) chrysoprase (green), heliotrope (dark green with red spots).—**Occurrence:** Nodules in limestone, concretions in weathering crusts, infillings in volcanic rocks.—**Localities:** For the jewellery trade useful pieces come from Brazil, Uruguay, Madagascar, India. Also very fine specimens have come from Cornwall.—**Uses:** Used for jewellery since ancient times. Presently worked for rings, necklaces, pendants and objets d'art. Frequently artificially coloured.—**Illustration:** Stalactitic chalcedony aggregate, Brazil.

Jasper (Quartz group)

SiO₂ Silicon oxide

Characteristics: Colours generally red, but yellow, brown, green and grey types occur, mainly streaked or flecked. Hardness about 6½. Spec. Gravity about 2.6. Opaque. Fracture splintery. No cleavage. Chalcedony is considered to be a separate group within the quartz family. Jasper contains iron oxides, which give the red colour, and as such is a mixture and not a true mineral species.—**Occurrence:** Found amongst certain metamorphic rocks.—**Localities:** Aberdaron, Caernarvonshire; near Edinburgh; Campsie Glen, Stirlingshire, also India; USSR; USA.—**Uses:** Objets d'art, mosaics, jewellery, such as rings and pendants. Depending on colour markings, locality of origin or setting it is known commercially by many names, which give the impession that it is a more valuable stone.—**Illustration:** Cut brecciated jasper, Australia.

Silicified Wood

SiO₂ Silicon oxide

Characteristics: Colour brown, grey, red, yellow, blue. Streak white, also coloured. Hardness 6½. Spec. Gravity about 2.6. Waxy lustre, opaque. Fracture uneven, splintery. No cleavage. Has the overall composition of chalcedony. All the original wood has been dissolved by circulating ground water and replaced by silica, but the structure of the wood may be preserved in great detail.—**Occurrence:** Formed only where fine-grained material such as clay or marl has covered and protected wood against decay soon after the death of the plant.—**Localities:** USA (Arizona; Nevada); Argentina (Patagonia); Egypt (near Cairo).—**Uses:** Coloured varieties as objets d'art. Also worked as jewellery.—**Illustration:** Polished silicified wood, Nevada, U.S.A.

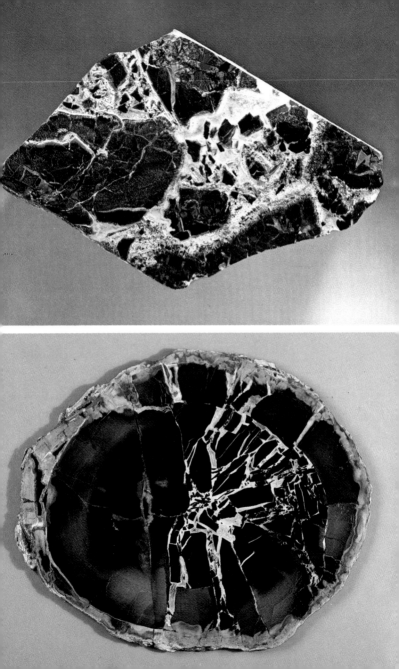

Agate (Quartz group)

SiO₂ *Silicon oxide*

Characteristics: Can show virtually all colours, always banded. The bands may be differently coloured or similar in tones. Streak white, hardness about 6½. Spec. Gravity about 2.6. Vitreous to waxy lustre, opaque. Translucent in thin slices. Fracture conchoidal. No cleavage. Usually forms approximately spherical masses. The bands are produced by rhythmic crystallisation. The individual bands run mostly parallel to the outer margin of the mass. In the interior there is occasionally a cavity in which well-formed crystals of quartz, amethyst, smoky quartz, calcite, hematite, siderite or zeolites can form.—**Occurrence:** Produced in silica poor volcanic rocks, such as basalt. Often found as isolated rounded lumps, produced by weathering of the igneous rock in which they were formed.—**Localities:** Cheddar, Somerset; Ayrshire; Forfarshire; Fife; and elsewhere in Scotland; Brazil (southern states); Uruguay; China; India; Madagascar; Mexico; U.S.A.—**Uses:** Used by the ancient Egyptians for jewellery, as cylinder seals and for containers. Nowadays also very popular for jewellery and objets d'art. By reason of its hardness and resistance to chemicals much used also in industry (pestles and mortars, bearings for balances, in the leather and paper industries, and for medical and chemical instruments). The agate from South America, the main source of supply for the world market, is usually not very strikingly coloured or marked. It is artificially coloured when cut so as to enhance the structure. According to pattern, markings and structure agate is known as eyed agate, banded agate, fortress agate etc.—**Illustration:** Above: Agate with graded bands from Uruguay (⅓ natural size). Below: Agate with central cavity from Mexico (⅔ natural size).

Opal   (Quartz group)

SiO$_2$ nH$_2$O   Water-bearing silicon oxide

Characteristics: Colour white, grey, blue, green, orange, red, black. Streak white. Hardness 5½-6½. Spec. Gravity 1.8-2.3. Vitreous to resinous lustre, may be pearly, transparent to sub-translucent. Fracture conchoidal, splintery. No cleavage. No crystals, amorphous. Aggregates botryoidal and rounded. Three varieties of opal are distinguished; schillerised, precious opal; yellow-red, transparent fire opal; and common opal. Precious opal with its rainbow play of colours (called opalescence) with changes according to the angle of viewing is the most coveted and also the rarest variety. The varieties with light background colours are known commercially as white opal, those with dark blue, dark green or grey-black body colours as black opal. Opal is easily damaged by heat, pressure and blows. By loss of the constituent water it alters, becomes splintery, and loses its opalescence. When saturated with oil the play of colours is temporarily enhanced; alteration can be arrested or at least slowed down by storage in damp cotton wool. Fire opal has no schiller, is orange to red in colour, and translucent to transparent. It is also liable to be damaged easily. Common opal has no play of colours. Opal is known commercially by many names, e.g. honey-milk-moss, wax and water opal. Occasionally the so-called petrified wood is composed of opal.—**Occurrence:** Thin layers from 1-2mm thick embedded in sandstone intergrown with the matrix. Occasionally fossils are also replaced by opal.—**Localities:** Found in a number of localities in Cornwall, also County Antrim, Ireland. Precious opal in Australia (New South Wales; South Australia; Queensland); Brazil; Japan; USA (Nevada). Formerly Czechoslovakia (Cervenica). Fire opal in Mexico; Brazil; Western Australia; Turkey. Common opal found world-wide.—**Uses:** Precious and fire opal as rounded slices for jewellery. Common opal for artistic objects.—**Illustration:** Opal in matrix, Australia.

Cerussite

PbCO₃   Lead carbonate

Characteristics: Colour white, colourless, yellow, grey, brown. Streak white to grey. Hardness 3-3½. Spec. Gravity 6.4-6.6. Adamantine lustre, transparent to translucent. Fracture conchoidal, uneven. Two distinct cleavages parallel to length of crystals. Crystals (orthorhombic system) distinct, tabular, columnar, acicular, frequently twinned.—**Occurrence:** Oxidised zones of lead-zinc sulphide ore deposits.—**Localities:** Formerly very fine crystals were found at Leadhills in Scotland; also Austria (Bleiberg); Czechoslovakia (Pribram; Mies, Bohemia); Sardinia; USSR (Kazakhstan; Altai); Zambia (Broken Hill); South West Africa (Tsumeb); USA (Arizona, Colorado).—**Uses:** Important ore of lead. Clear crystals are occasionally cut by collectors.—**Illustration:** Cerussite group from Tsumeb, South West Africa.

Azurite

Cu₃ (CO₃)₂ (OH)₂   Basic copper carbonate

Characteristics: Colour various shades of deep blue. Streak light blue. Hardness 3½-4. Spec. Gravity 3.8-3.9. Vitreous lustre, transparent to opaque. Fracture conchoidal. Cleavage perfect, dissolves easily in acids. Cystals (monoclinic system) frequently short prismatic, interpenetrating, thick tabular, richly facetted. Aggregates dense, earthy, reniform, as coatings.—**Occurrence:** Together with malachite in copper ore deposits or nearby, but also disposed as spherical aggregates. Occasionally intergrown with malachite.—**Localities:** Found in many of the old mines in Cornwall, and in the Bridgwater area, Somerset; also USSR (Urals; Altai); USA (Arizona, Pennsylvania); Australia; Chile; Mexico.—**Uses:** Formerly for azure pigment, nowadays principally as a source of copper. Also for objets d'art. Occasionally cut by collectors. Easily damaged by reason of its low hardness.—**Illustration:** Dark blue azurite with some green malchite from Tsumeb, South West Africa.

Dolomite

CaMg (CO₃)₂   Calcium magnesium carbonate

$CaMg (CO_3)_2$ *Calcium magnesium carbonate*

Characteristics: Colour white, yellowish, brown, rarely colourless. Streak white. Hardness 3½-4. Spec. Gravity 2.8-2.9. Vitreous to pearly lustre, translucent, rarely transparent. Fracture subconchoidal. Cleavage perfect, breaks to form 6-sided⁻ rhombs. Crystals (trigonal system) distinct and intergrown, frequently curved and saddle shaped. Rarely twinned. Aggregates dense, granular, fibrous, cellular-porous, frequently associated with calcite. Will dissolve in warm dilute hydrochloric acid, with effervescence.—**Occurrence:** In veins and joints, main constituent of dolomitic limestone.—**Localities:** Durham, Cumbria and the Isle of Man; Germany (Saxony; Freiberg); Switzerland (Binnental; Italy (Dolomites).—**Uses:** As a flux in the smelting of iron, as refractory material, in the chemical industry. As road metal, as a building stone as well as an additive for various other building materials.—**Illustration:** Dolomite group encrusted with colourless calcite, Durham, England.

Aragonite

CaCO₃   Calcium carbonate

$CaCO_3$ *Calcium carbonate*

Characteristics: Colour grey, yellowish, white, reddish, bluish, colourless. Streak white. Hardness 3½-4. Spec. Gravity 2.9. Vitreous lustre, greasy lustre on broken surfaces, transparent to translucent. Fracture subconchoidal. Cleavage imperfect. Crystals (orthorhombic system) stout prisms usually twinned. Aggregates radiating, in parallel fibres, acicular, branching, and encrusting.—**Occurrence:** Ore deposits, joints, cavities. Does not form large rock complexes. Snow-white branching forms, so called flos-ferri, found in siderite deposits. Layered or rounded aggregates (pea stones) formed by precipitation from spring water. Aragonite is also the constituent material of some sea shells and pearls.—**Localities:** Groups of acicular crystals have come from a number of localities in Cumbria; also Czechoslovakia (Carlsbad); Italy (Sicily); Spain (Aragon).—**Uses:** Interpenetration twins and flos-ferri sought by collectors.—**Illustration:** Flos-ferri from Erzberg, Steiermark, Austria.

Calcite

CaCO₃ Calcium carbonate

Characteristics: Colour white, grey, yellow, reddish, brownish, green, colourless. Streak white, coloured when impure. Hardness 3. Spec. Gravity 2.7. Vitreous lustre, transparent, to translucent. Fracture conchoidal but rarely seen because of good cleavage. Cleavage perfect. Readily broken to form characteristic rhomb shapes. Crystals (trigonal system) predominantly rhombohedra, scalenohedra and prisms, many combinations, frequently twinned. Large crystals in joints and cavities. Aggregates fine-grained, columnar, platy, fibrous. Dissolves readily, with effervescence, in dilute hydrochloric acid.—**Occurrence:** Principal component of limestone, in numerous sandstones as grains or as a cement, in metamorphic rocks, in ore veins, as stalactites and stalagmites.—**Localities:** A common mineral found in many places. Fine crystals have come from Cumbria, Lancashire, Durham, Derbyshire and Cornwall.—**Uses:** Iceland spar, a colourless, clear variety of calcite with marked birefringence, for optical instruments. Calcite is facetted by collectors.—**Illustration:** Calcite group with steep rhombohedra, Grimmelshofen, Black Forest, Germany.

Rhodochrosite

MnCO₃ Manganese carbonate

Characteristics: Colour rose-red to grey, becomes partially brown on exposure to air. Streak white. Hardness 3½-4½. Spec. Gravity 3.4-3.7. Vitreous lustre, pearly lustre on cleavage surfaces, translucent. Fracture uneven. Three perfect cleavages. Crystals (trigonal system) rare and mostly small; rhombohedra, often distorted into lensoid shapes, only in cavities. Aggregates compact, massive, earthy, fibrous, radiating, banded red and white with zigzag patterns.—**Occurrence:** In veins and as stalagmites.—**Localities:** St. Just and Botallack, Cornwall; also Spain (Huelva); Italy (Elba); France (Pyrenees); USSR (Urals; Transcaucasia). Material suitable for jewellery in Argentina (east of Mendoza and south of Tucuman); also in USA (Colorado; Montana).—**Uses:** Important ore of manganese. Since 1950 in commerce as a gemstone.—**Illustration:** Cut rhodochrosite stalagmites, Argentina.

Siderite chalybite

FeCO₃ Iron carbonate

Characteristics: Colour, yellow to dark brown, grey. Streak white, brown to black in weathered material. Hardness 3½-4½. Spec. Gravity 3.8-4.0. Vitreous lustre, transparent to translucent. Fracture uneven. Three perfect cleavages. Crystals (trigonal system) mainly rhombohedra, frequently with curved faces. Aggregates compact, fine and coarse-grained, radiating, botryoidal.—**Occurrence:** In veins and layers, lenses, spherical concretions and ooliths. When mixed with clay forms clay ironstone.—**Localities:** Fine specimens have come from Tavistock in Devon and from many of the mines in Cornwall; also Scotland; Austria (Erzberg); Spain (Bilbao); USA (Connecticut; Idaho); USSR (Urals).—**Uses:** Important ore of iron, of great use for special steels.—**Illustration:** Siderite group with white calcite from Neudorf, Harz, Germany.

Smithsonite

ZnCO₃ Zinc carbonate

Characteristics: Colour grey, white, brown, green, blue, pink. Streak white. Hardness 4-4½. Spec. Gravity 4.3-4.5. Vitreous lustre, translucent. Fracture uneven, brittle. Cleavage perfect. Crystals (trigonal system) very rare and small rhombohedra. Faces frequently rough and curved. Aggregates granular, stalactitic, compact in botryoidal or porous cellular masses, encrusting.—**Occurrence:** In veins and cavities, as crusts in limestone or dolomite.—**Localities:** Alston Moor, Cumbria, and at Matlock in Derbyshire; Italy (Sardinia); Greece (Laurium); Northern Spain; Mexico (Boléo); South West Africa (Tsumeb); USA (Arkansas; Colorado; Utah).—**Uses:** Important ore of zinc. Light coloured varieties as jewellery and for artistic objects.—**Illustration:** Botryoidal smithsonite group from Kelly Mine, New Mexico, USA.

Malachite

Cu₂CO₃(OH)₂   *Basic copper carbonate*

$Cu_2CO_3(OH)_2$ *Basic copper carbonate*

Characteristics: Colour emerald-green, dark green. Streak light green. Hardness 3½-4. Spec. Gravity 3.7-4.0. In natural specimens weak vitreous lustre or dull, silky lustre on freshly broken or cut surfaces, translucent to opaque. Fracture sub-conchoidal, uneven scaly. Cleavage perfect. Crystals (monoclinic system) very rare. Aggregates, finely fibrous, radiating, rounded nodules, with forms similar to hematite; stalactitic, rarely in platy crusts and as coatings, occasionally earthy. Typically banded in light and dark layers which show on cut surfaces as concentric rings and parallel stripes. It is rarely possible to obtain large uniformly coloured pieces. Sensitive to heat and dissolves in dilute hydrochloric acid. Often occurs together with azurite and with turquoise and chrysocolla.—**Occurrence:** In or near copper ore deposits.—**Localities:** Has come from a number of the mining areas in Cornwall. Formerly large amounts at Sverdlovsk in the Urals where pieces over 50 metric tons in weight were obtained. Presently main production in Zaire (Katanga); Australia; Chile; Rhodesia; South West Africa (Tsumeb); USA (Arizona).—**Uses:** Widespread ore of copper. In the past for jewellery, and amulets; when powdered used as eyeshadow. Also used nowadays for jewellery and as a decorative stone in spite of its inferior hardness. Also worked for beads, and cabochons and mounted for brooches, pendants and necklaces, and also used for wall decorations; also for objets d'art e.g. plates, boxes, vases, figures. The cutter must try to make the most decorative expression of the natural banding of the malachite.—**Illustration:** Malachite aggregate with typical banding, Katanga, Zaire (⅔ natural size).

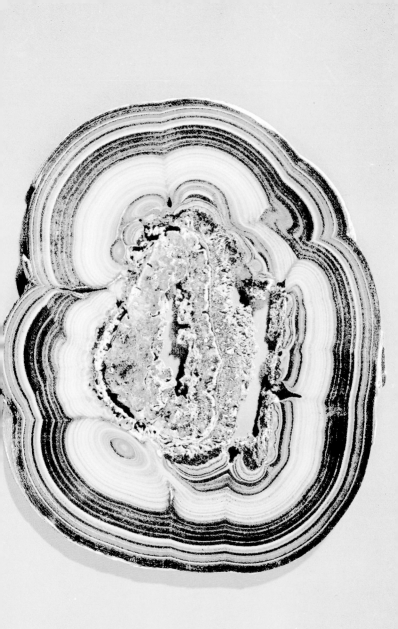

Celestine

Sr SO₄   *Strontium sulphate*

Characteristics: Colour bluish white, white, colourless, rarely reddish, yellowish or green. Streak white. Hardness 3-3½. Spec. Gravity 3.9-4.0. Vitreous lustre, pearly lustre on cleavage surfaces, transparent to translucent. Fracture uneven. Cleavage perfect across crystals, good parallel to their length. Crystals (orthorhombic system) often richly facetted, columnar, rarely tabular. Aggregates granular, or fibrous.—**Occurrence:** In joints and veins, frequently in cavities.—**Localities:** Found in nodules in sedimentary rocks around Yate, Gloucestershire. Also Austria (Salzburg); Italy (Agrigento; Sicily); Spain (Granada); USA (Tennessee); USSR (Archangel; Transcaspian).—**Uses:** For fireworks and flares (it gives a bright red flame), in the sugar industry (purification of molasses), and the glass industry. Cut and polished by collectors.—**Illustration:** Celestine group in cavity, Madagascar.

Crocoite

PbCrO₄   *Lead chromate*

Characteristics: Colour yellow-red, red-orange. The colour fades gradually on exposure to light. Streak orange-yellow. Hardness 2½-3. Spec. Gravity 5.9-6.1. Adamantine to vitreous lustre, translucent. Fracture uneven. Cleavage distinct along length of crystals. Crystals (monoclinic system) common, prismatic, acicular. Aggregates massive; granular.—**Occurrence:** Very occasionally in oxidation zones of lead-bearing ore deposits. Crystals only in cavities. Associated minerals are galena, cerussite, and pyromorphite.—**Localities:** USSR (Ural Mountains); Tasmania (Dundas district), Philippines (Luzon), Brazil (Goyabeira).—**Uses:** No economic uses because of its rarity. Sought by collectors as a rarity, even cut and polished.—**Illustration:** Crocoite group from Australia.

Wulfenite

PbMoO₄   Lead molybdate

Characteristics: Colour wax or honey yellow, orange, grey, brown, rarely colourless. Streak white. Hardness 3. Spec. Gravity 6.5-7.0. Adamantine to resinous lustre, transparent to subtranslucent. Fracture subconchoidal, uneven. Cleavage distinct. Crystals (tetragonal system) mainly distinct, thin plates, rarely bipyramidal forms. Aggregates compact, granular, but rare.—**Occurrence:** In oxidation zone of lead ore deposits.—**Localities:** Has been found at Priddy in Somerset; Austria (Bleiberg); Yugoslavia (Carniola); Czechoslovakia (Pribram); USA (Utah; Arizona); South West Africa (Tsumeb).—**Uses:** Important ore of molybdenum. Molybdenum is used as an additive for high quality steel, and as a catalyst. Beautifully coloured crystals are cut and polished by collectors.—**Illustration:** Wulfenite group of thin platy crystals from Bleiberg, Karnten, Austria.

Baryte, Barytes, Heavy Spar

BaSO₄   Barium sulphate

Characteristics: Colour whitish, grey, yellow, reddish, rarely colourless. Streak white, Hardness 2½-3½. Spec. Gravity 4.3-4.6. Vitreous lustre, transparent to translucent. Fracture uneven, brittle. Cleavages perfect and very good. Crystals (orthorhombic system) tabular, often with many faces. Aggregates granular, dense, reniform, stalactitic, leafy or in rosettes (baryte roses).—**Occurrence:** In veins and as non-ore mineral in sulphide, and iron ore deposits, occasionally as concretions.—**Localities:** Crystals often very large, were found in the Dufton lead mines in Westmorland; also in Shropshire and at a number of localities in Cornwall.—**Uses:** By reason of its high specific gravity as a filler for paper and textiles, as drilling mud in oil drilling, as a radiation shield in X-ray laboratories, as a glaze and filler for art paper. Extensively used in the chemical industry. Formerly used as a white pigment.—**Illustration:** Baryte group with cerussite, Morocco.

Gypsum

$CaSO_4 . 2H_2O$ Hydrated calcium sulphate

Characteristics: Colour white, colourless, other colours also as a result of impurities, mainly however only light tones. Streak white. Hardness 1½-2, Spec. Gravity 2.2-2.4. Vitreous lustre, pearly lustre on cleavage surfaces, transparent to opaque. Fracture conchoidal, inelastic. Cleavage perfect. Crystals (monoclinic system) common, distinct or intergrown, mainly prismatic-tabular, also bent and lens-shaped. Interpenetration and contact twins (swallow tail twins). Aggregates dense, granular, acicular, fibrous as parallel fibres (satin spar), dense (alabaster). Often contains bitumen or clay as impurities.—**Occurrence:** Chiefly in evaporite deposits with halite and anhydrite (calcium sulphate, $CaSO_4$ i.e. similar to gypsum but without the water), or by the hydration of anhydrite. Occasionally also in loose sand (desert roses).—**Localities:** Found at Nantwich, Cheshire; satin spar from Matlock, Derbyshire; crystals in clay at Shotover Hill, near Oxford.—**Uses:** In the building industry as material for Stucco work and plaster for putty and cement; for light building material, in the paper industry, as a filler in the manufacture of paint, for plaster casts and orthopaedic plaster. Alabaster as a sculpting medium and for objets d'art.—**Illustration:** Gypsum group, Berchtesgaden, Bavaria, Germany. (about ⅔ natural size).

Desert Rose,   Sand Rose, Gypsum Rose

Characteristics: Desert roses are formed from thin platy crystals of gypsum which, sometimes are arranged round a central point, similar to the petals of a rose. The individual rosettes are linked to form large groups. Desert roses arise from the deposition of gypsum, and more rarely baryte, in loose sand, where they can develop unhindered in all directions. The sand grains become incorporated in the crystals and give them a yellowish, brownish or reddish colour and also a granular roughness.—**Localities:** The Moroccan, Algerian and Tunisian Sahara; USA (Norman; Oklahoma). Desert roses are occasionally called Sahara-roses, or Texas roses after the localities at which they are found.—**Illustration:** Desert rose from the Sahara.

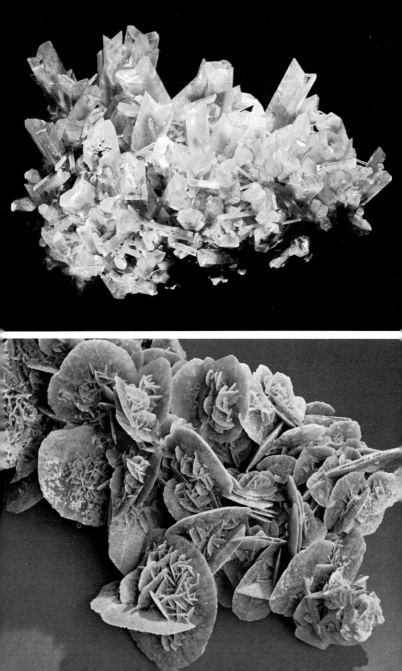

Wavellite

$Al_3 (OH)_3 (PO_4)_2 . 5H_2O$ Hydrated aluminium phosphate

Characteristics: Colour, grey, yellowish, greenish, colourless. Streak white to light grey. Hardness 3½-4. Spec. Gravity 2.3-2.4. Vitreous lustre, translucent. fracture uneven, brittle. Cleavage good parallel to length of crystals. Crystals (orthorhombic system) thin, acicular. Aggregates characteristically globular masses of fibrous, radiating crystals.—**Occurrence:** In joints and cavities of siliceous and argillaceous rocks (particularly siliceous schists and greywacke) and in cavities in phosphatic rocks. Associated minerals are hematite, limonite, pyrolusite.—**Localities:** Wavellite was first described from a locality near Barnstaple, Devon; also from Cornwall and County Cork, Ireland; Brazil; Bolivia.—**Uses:** Only sporadically worked as a phosphate.—**Illustration:** Fibrous radiating wavellite aggregate from Brazil.

Pyromorphite

$Pb_5 Cl (PO_4)_3 Cl$ Chlorine containing lead phosphate

Characteristics: Colour green, yellow, brown, white, colourless, rarely reddish. Streak white. Hardness 3½-4. Spec. Gravity 6.5-7.1. Resinous lustre, transparent to translucent. Fracture subconchoidal. No cleavage. Crystals (hexagonal system) simple prismatic forms, usually barrel-shaped, occasionally also acicular. Aggregates as cavity linings or dense, botryoidal, granular or as crusts or coatings.—**Occurrence:** In oxidised zones of lead-zinc sulphide ore deposits. Associated minerals are baryte, galena, cerussite, limonite.—**Localities:** Fine crystals have come from Roughton Gill, Cumbria; also from Cornwall and Leadhills, Lanarkshire; Czechoslovakia (Pribram); USSR (Urals; Transbaikalia); Zambia (Broken Hill).—**Uses:** Important ore of lead, but rarely in large concentrations.—**Illustration:** Pyromorphite group from Schaninsland, Black Forest, Germany (Magnified 8 times).

Turquoise

$CuAl_6[(OH)_2PO_4]_4 . 4H_2O$ Cupriferous basic aluminium phosphate

Characteristics: Colour sky-blue, blue-green, apple-green. Streak white or greenish. Hardness 5-6. Spec. Gravity 2.6-2.8. Usually a waxy lustre, crystals vitreous; opaque. Fracture uneven. Cleavage imperfect along length of crystals. Crystals (triclinic system) very small and rare. Until small crystals were first found in 1911, turquoise was thought to be amorphous. Aggregates dense, botryoidal, reniform encrusting or in veins.—**Occurrence:** As joint infillings, botryoidal overgrowths, or as nodules in aluminous rocks. Most are penetrated by brown or black net-like veins.—**Localities:** Iran (Nischapur); Afghanistan; Israel (Eilat); Australia; Tibet; Tanzania; USA (Nevada; Colorado).—**Uses:** For jewellery usually as cabochons (necklaces, rings, brooches) and for objets d'art. Turquoise deposits were being worked in the Sinai peninsula in 4000 B.C.—**Illustration:** Turquoise on matrix and cabochon, Nevada, USA.

Apatite

$Ca_5(PO_4)_3(F, Cl, OH)$ calcium phosphate containing fluorine and chlorine

Characteristics: Colour yellow, green, blue, violet, pink, colourless. Streak white. Hardness 5. Spec. Gravity 3.1-3.3. Vitreous to subresinous lustre, transparent to translucent. Fracture conchoidal, uneven. Cleavage imperfect across length of crystals. Crystals (hexagonal system) short and long prisms or thick plates with rounded edges, often very large. Aggregates compact, granular, fibrous, botryoidal and earthy.—**Occurrence:** Large crystals in cavities. In pegmatites and a wide range of igneous and metamorphic rocks in which it is a common mineral. As nodules in sedimentary rocks.—**Localities:** Found at Carrock Fell, Cumbria, associated with the tin ores of Cornwall, and at various localities in Devon; Sweden (Alnö); USSR (Kola Peninsula; Ukraine); USA (Maine; Idaho; Utah); and at many other localities.—**Uses:** Mainly as fertilizer, also in the chemical industry (phosphoric acid). Beautifully coloured varieties cut and polished as gemstones.—**Illustration:** Apatite group overgrown by quartz, Mexico.

Vanadinite

Pb₅(VO₄)₃Cl   *Lead chloro-vanadate*

Characteristics: Colour brown, orange to red. Streak light yellow to white. Hardness 3. Spec. Gravity 6.7-7.1. Resinous lustre, transparent to subtranslucent. Fracture subconchoidal. No cleavage. Crystals (hexagonal system) small, short columnar, acicular, prismatic, occasionally hollow.—**Occurrence:** In weathering zones of lead ore deposits. Associated minerals are descloizite, pyromorphite, wulfenite.—**Localities:** Found at Leadhills, Lanarkshire and Wanlockhead, Dumfries, Scotland; Potts Gill, Cumberland; Yugoslavia (Mies); Spain (Sierra Nevada); Zambia (Broken Hill); South West Africa (Tsumeb); Mexico; USA (Arizona; Colorado; New Mexico).—**Uses:** Important ore of vanadium. Vanadium is an alloying metal for hard, heat and acid resistant and rustproof steels, also used for the production of catalysts and of dyestuffs.—**Illustration:** Group of vanadinite crystals, Morocco (about twice natural size).

Descloizite

Pb(Zn, Cu) VO₄ (OH).   *Lead, zinc, copper vanadate*

Characteristics: Colour brown, brown-red, black. Streak orange to brownish red. Hardness 3½. Spec. Gravity 5.9-6.2. Greasy to adamantine lustre, translucent. Fracture conchoidal. No cleavage. Crystals (orthorhombic system) bipyramidal, prismatic or tabular, faces uneven and rough. Aggregates mamillated with fibrous radiating structure, also encrusting and stalactitic. Associated minerals are cerussite, limonite, mimetite, pyromorphite, quartz, vanadinite.—**Occurrence:** In the weathering zones of lead-copper-zinc ore deposits, also in sandstones.—**Localities:** A variety of descloizite is found at Alderley Edge and at Mottram, both in Cheshire; also at Brandy Gill, Cumbria; South West Africa (Tsumeb); Zambia (Broken Hill); Zaire (Katanga); USA (Arizona; New Mexico).—**Uses:** An ore of vanadium which is used as an alloying metal for heat and acid resistant steels. —**Illustration:** Descloizite group from South West Africa.

Variscite

AlPO₄. 2H₂O   Hydrated aluminium phosphate

Characteristics: Colour yellow-green, apple-green, bluish, nearly colourless. Streak white. Hardness 3.5-4.5. Spec. Gravity 2.4-2.6. Waxy lustre, opaque to translucent. Fracture conchoidal, brittle. Crystals (orthorhombic system) octahedral, small and very rare. Aggregates fine-grained, as crusts or nodules, reniform.—**Occurrence:** In veins and joints in metamorphic rocks; e.g. siliceous schists.—**Localities:** Devon; Austria (Leoben, Steiermark), USA (Utah; Nevada; Arkansas); Australia (Queensland).—**Uses:** For jewellery with cabochon cut, for objets d'art and as an ornamental stone.— **Illustration:** Cut and polished variscite aggregate, Perth, Australia.

Mimetite

Pb₅(AsO₄)₃Cl   Lead chloro-arsenate

Characteristics: Colour mainly honey-yellow, also colourless, grey, greenish, brown. Streak white. Hardness 3½-4. Spec. Gravity 7.0-7.2. Resinous lustre, translucent to subtransparent. fracture subconchoidal. No cleavage. Crystals (hexagonal system) barrel-shaped, tabular, short columnar and also prismatic, acicular. Aggregates botryoidal, earthy, in crusts and cavities.—**Occurrence:** Weathering zones of lead-zinc sulphide ore deposits which carry arsenic.—**Localities:** Found at a number of localities in Cornwall and Cumbria; Czechoslovakia (Pribram); South West Africa (Tsumeb); USA (Tintic, Utah); Mexico (Santa Eulalia).—**Uses:** Because of its rarity, unimportant economically. Sought by collectors. —**Illustration:** Mimetite from Tsumeb, South West Africa. The large crystal to the right is over 2cm long.

Kyanite   Disthene
Al₂SiO₅   Aluminium silicate

Al_2SiO_5

Characteristics: Colour blue, blue-green, colourless, occasionally white, colours often unevenly distributed, darkest shades being in the centre of crystals or in patches. Streak white. Hardness along the length of crystals 5½, across the crystals 6-7. The name disthene derives from this; it means "providing twofold resistance". Spec. Gravity 3.5-3.7. Vitreous lustre, pearly lustre on cleavage, surfaces transparent to translucent. Fracture fibrous, brittle. Two good cleavages. Crystals (triclinic system) mainly intergrown, long flat prisms, broad-bladed, resembling a ruler, sometimes bent and with cross-striations. Aggregates radiating. Not soluble in acids.—**Occurrence:** As a constituent of metamorphic rocks, mainly in mica schists, sometimes forms monomineralic layers or pods. Occasionally in cavities and alluvial deposits. Associated minerals are andalusite, mica, corundum, rutile, staurolite, tourmaline.—**Localities:** At various places in the Scottish Highlands, and fine groups of crystals are found in the Shetland Islands; also Switzerland (many localities); Yugoslavia (Prilipec); Norway (Rognan); Sweden (Varmland); Finland (North Karelia); USSR (Kola Peninsula); USA (California; North Carolina; Virginia); India (Assam); Burma; Brazil (Minas Gerais); Kenya (Machakos); Western Australia (Mt. Margaret).—**Uses:** Kyanite-bearing rocks are worked for the manufacture of refractory and acid resistant products. Strongly coloured specimens in the gemstone industry, but difficult to cut and polish by reason of the differential hardness and good cleavage.—**Illustration:** Kyanite crystals in mica schist, Pizzo Forno, Tessin, Switzerland.

Aquamarine (Beryl group)

$Be_3Al_2Si_6O_{18}$ *Aluminium beryllium silicate*

Characteristics: Colour light blue, blue, blue-green; colour distribution not always homogeneous. Streak white: Hardness 7½-8. Spec. Gravity 2.6-2.8. Vitreous lustre, transparent to opaque. Fracture conchoidal to uneven, brittle. Poor cleavage. Crystals (hexagonal system) often large, long, columnar, six sided prisms. Aggregates in compact masses, but rare. Aquamarine and emerald (see below) are not distinct mineral species but varieties of the mineral beryl and distinguished by their colour only.—**Occurrence:** In pegmatites and coarse-grained granites, partly also in alluvial deposits.—**Localities:** Mourne Mountains, County Down; Brazil (many states); Madagascar; USA (many states); USSR (Urals; Transbaikalia).—**Uses:** As gemstone, mainly with step and bevelled cuts in rectangular or long elliptical forms. The most prized are large deeply coloured stones, the commonest are of a pale sea-green colour. On heating to about 400°C the greenish colour changes to a bluish tone.—**Illustration:** Aquamarine crystal in quartz, Brazil.

Emerald (Beryl group)

$Be_3Al_2Si_6O_{18}$ *Aluminium beryllium silicate*

Characteristics: Colour emerald green, yellowish green, dark green. Disposition of colour may be irregular. Streak white. Hardness 7½-8. Spec. Gravity 2.6-2.8. Vitreous lustre, transparent to opaque. Fracture conchoidal to uneven, brittle. Poor cleavage. Crystals (hexagonal system) long six-sided prisms. Aggregates compact, but rare.—**Occurrence:** Intergrown in pegmatite dykes and in schists, or as distinct crystals on the walls of cavities, partly also in alluvial deposits.—**Localities:** The world's finest emeralds come from near Muso, north-east of Bogota, Colombia; also from Brazil (Bahia; Goias; Minas Gerais); Rhodesia; South Africa (Transvaal).-—**Uses:** As a gemstone for jewellery, e.g. rings, pendants, necklaces; also for engraving and objets d'art.—**Illustration:** Emerald in matrix, Brazil.

Epidote   Pistacite

$Ca_2(Al, Fe)_3 Si_3 O_{12}(OH)$.   Calcium-aluminium-iron silicate

Characteristics: Colour dark green, blue-green, black-brown. Streak grey. Hardness 6-7. Spec. Gravity 3.2-3.5. Vitreous lustre, transparent to nearly opaque. Fracture uneven, splintery. One perfect cleavage parallel to length of crystals. Crystals (monoclinic system) striated along their length, prismatic, richly facetted. Aggregates compact, radiating, often grouped in clusters. The light green and green-brown iron-poor variety is called clinozoisite. An opaque, cherry-red and manganiferous variety from Piedmont in Italy and elsewhere is called piemontite.—**Occurrence:** In cavities and on joints in metamorphic rocks.—**Localities:** Near Ivybridge, Devonshire, and in the Scottish Highlands; Switzerland (Zermatt); Norway; USSR (Southern Urals); USA (Alaska; California); Mexico; Mozambique.—**Uses:** Occasionally cut and polished by collectors.—**Illustration:** Epidote group, Baja, Mexico.

Rhodonite

(Mn, Ca, Fe) SiO_3 Manganese silicate

Characteristics: Colour flesh pink to dark red, rarely brown-red, with black flecks or veins of manganese oxide. Streak white. Hardness 5½-6½. Spec. Gravity 3.5-3.7. Vitreous lustre, pearly lustre on cleavage surfaces, translucent to transparent. Fracture uneven to conchoidal, brittle. Three cleavages: Two perfect and one good. Crystals (triclinic system) prismatic, rare and usually badly formed, platy. Aggregates compact, granular, dense.—**Occurrence:** In thick layers in argillaceous and metamorphic rocks. Associated minerals are braunite, calcite, franklinite, hausmannite, manganite, willemite, zincite.—**Localities:** Meldon, Devon; Several localities in Cornwall; also Anglesey; Sweden (Varm), and USSR (Urals); USA (New Jersey); Mexico; Canada (Vancouver Island); Australia (New South Wales); India.—**Uses:** Important ore of manganese. Beautifully coloured varieties worked for jewellery, objets d'art and as wall decoration.—**Illustration:** Cut and polished rhodonite aggregate, Franklin, New Jersey, USA.

Lapis Lazuli   Lazurite

(Na, Ca)$_8$ (Al, Si)$_{12}$ O$_{24}$ (S, SO$_4$)   Sulphur-bearing sodium aluminium silicate

Characteristics: Colour azure-blue. Streak light blue. Hardness 5-5½. Spec. Gravity 2.4-2.9. Vitreous lustre, opaque. Fracture uneven. No cleavage. Crystals (cubic system) very rare, cubes or octahedra. Aggregates granular or dense. Because other minerals are nearly always present in lapis lazuli, it is a rock rather than a mineral. The name lazurite refers to the blue mineral which is the principal constituent and is not a synonym. Sensitive to high pressures and temperatues. Most examples contain finely distributed pyrite and calcite pockets and veins.—**Occurrence:** Irregular layers in limestone and dolomitic marble.—**Localities:** Afghanistan (Hindukush Mountains): USSR (Lake Baikal area); Chile (Coquimbo Province).—**Uses:** Since prehistoric times for jewellery. Jasper coloured with Berlin Blue is known commercially as German or Swiss Lapis.—**Illustration:** Natural and cut and polished ring stone of lapis lazuli from Afghanistan.

Muscovite   (Mica group)

KAl$_2$ (AlSi$_3$O$_{10}$) (OH, F)$_2$ Potassium aluminium silicate

Characteristics: Colour colourless, pale red yellow or pale green. Streak white. Hardness 2½-3. Spec. Gravity 2.8-2.9. Pearly, silvery metallic lustre, thin flakes tansparent, otherwise translucent. One perfect cleavage, splits easily into thin flakes, flexible, elastic, heat and acid resistant, resistant to weathering. Crystals (monoclinic system) tabular, platy, occasionally columnar. Aggregates platy with irregular outlines.—**Occurrence:** Important mineral of many rocks. Large muscovite plates common in pegmatite veins.—**Localities:** Cornwall; Cumbria; Banffshire, Aberdeen, and Argyll, Scotland; Switzerland (St. Gotthard); Norway; USSR (Urals; Eastern Siberia); India (Bengal; Madras); USA (North Carolina; Maryland); and many other localities.—**Uses:** As an insulator in the electrical industry, as a fireproof material in the construction industry and for ovens and furnaces. Formerly called "Muscovy Glass".-- **Illustration:** Platy muscovite group, Urals.

Zoisite

Ca$_2$ Al$_3$ Si$_3$ O$_{12}$ (OH)   Calcium aluminium silicate

Characteristics: Colour grey, yellowish, greenish, blue, colourless. Streak white. Hardness 6-7. Spec. Gravity 3.2-3.4. Pearly to vitreous lustre, transparent to subtranslucent. Fracture uneven, brittle. One perfect cleavage. Crystals (orthorhombic system) prismatic, often striated and sharply bent, well-developed end faces rare. Aggregates compact, bladed, fibrous A dense red to pink variety is called thulite.—**Occurrence:** In metamorphosed calcium-bearing. rocks—**Localities:** From the Loch Garve area, Scotland; Switzerland (Wallis); Norway; Tanzania.—**Uses:** The sapphire to amethyst blue variety from Tanzania is a prized gemstone which first came on the market in 1967. It is called tanzanite after the country of Tanzania. Thulite is worked into cabochons and used as an ornamental stone.—**Illustration:** Amethyst coloured tanzanite in matrix and sapphire-blue tanzanite, both from Tanzania.

Prehnite

Ca$_2$ Al$_2$ Si$_3$ O$_{10}$ (OH)$_2$ Basic calcium aluminium silicate

Characteristics: Colour yellow-green, brownish yellow, white, colourless. Streak white. Hardness 6-6½. Spec. Gravity 2.9-3.0. Vitreous lustre, transparent to translucent. Fracture uneven. Cleavage good. Crystals (orthorhombic system) tabular, rarely with well developed faces. Twinned. aggregates fan-shaped and foliated like double-bladed axes, scaly, reniform, spherical. Occasionally prehnite replaces other minerals in which case it is called a pseudomorph of prehnite after, for example, analcime, laumontite or natrolite..—**Occurrence:** On joints and in cavities of certain igneous and metamorphic rocks. Associated minerals are calcite, epidote, zèolites.—**Localities:** Campsie Hills, Kilpatrick Hills, and Corstorphine Hill near Edinburgh, all in Scotland; Botallack, Cornwall; USA (New Jersey); South Africa.—**Uses:** Translucent prehnite of uniform colour as cabochons; it is sometimes facetted.—**Illustration:** Pseudomorph of prehnite after laumontite, Poonah, India.

Adularia (Feldspar group)
K AlSi₃O₈ *Potassium aluminium silicate*

Characteristics: Colour white, colourless, also pale yellow or green. Streak white. Hardness 6. Spec. Gravity 2.6. Vitreous lustre, sometimes pearly lustre, translucent to opaque. Fracture conchoidal to uneven. Two perfect cleavages. Crystals (monoclinic system) prisms terminated by two faces; very distinctive, frequently twinned, large crystals known. A pale milky variety with a blue-white opalescent schiller is called moonstone.—**Occurrence:** On joints in metamorphic rocks, often including or overgrown by chlorite.—**Localities:** In many places in the Alps, e.g. Switzerland (Wallis, St. Gotthard Massif); Austria (Tauern); moonstone of gem quality chiefly in Ceylon, also Australia; Brazil; Madagascar; USA.—**Uses:** Sought by collectors as a characteristic example of an alpine vein mineral. Moonstone is cut and polished as cabochons for jewellery.—**Illustration:** Adularia group, Wallis, Switzerland.

The feldspars comprise two sub-groups of the following minerals:-

Potassium feldspar

Orthoclase with the varieties adularia (a variety of which is moonstone) and sanidine. Microcline with the variety amazonstone.

Sodium-calcium feldspars

(also called plagioclase) albite, oligoclase, with the variety sunstone, andesine, labradorite, bytownite, anorthite.

Amazonstone (Feldspar group)

K AlSi₃ O₈ $KAlSi_3O_8$ *Potassium aluminium silicate*

Characteristics: Colour green, bluish-green. Streak white. Hardness 6-6½. Spec. Gravity 2.5-2.6. Vitreous lustre, weak pearly lustre on cleavage surfaces, opaque. Fracture conchoidal to uneven. Two perfect cleavages. Crystals (triclinic system) short prismatic, very large crystals known. Aggregates coarsely crystalline. Amazonstone is the green coloured variety of the feldspar 'microcline'.—**Occurrence:** In pegmatites associated particularly with granites. Associated minerals are albite, mica and quartz.—**Localities:** Has been found near Tongue, Sutherland, Scotland; USA (Colorado; Virginia; Pennsylvania); USSR (Urals); Brazil; India; Madagascar; South West Africa. Erroneously named after the Amazon region of South America, where it does not occur.—**Uses:** For jewellery, either facetted or as cabochons; as rounded forms for rings, brooches and necklaces and also for objets d'art. Probably used in ancient Egypt for jewellery and as a talisman.—**Illustration:** Amazonstone crystal on matrix, Colorado, USA.

Labradorite   Plagioclase (Feldspar group)

Composition half way between Na Al Si₃O₈ (albite) and Ca Al₂ Si₂ O₈ (anorthite).   Sodium-calcium aluminium silicate

Characteristics: Colour grey, white, bluish, black, often with play of colours chiefly in blues and greens but also in other colours. Streak white. Hardness 6-6½. Spec. Gravity 2.7. Vitreous to pearly, transparent to translucent. Fracture uneven. Two good cleavages. Crystals (triclinic system) tabular or prismatic. Aggregates compact.—**Occurrence:** Predominantly in igneous rocks such as gabbro, and certain metamorphic rocks.—**Localities:** Canada (Labrador; Newfoundland); Madagascar; Mexico; USA; USSR. A variety first discovered in the 1940's from Finland (Ylijärvi, Karelia) with an exceptionally clear play of colours is called spectrolite.—**Uses:** For jewellery (necklaces, brooches, rings), for objets d'art and as wall facing.—**Illustration:** Labradorite aggregate, Antsirabe, Madagascar.

Chrysocolla

CuSiO₃2H₂O   Hydrated copper silicate

$CuSiO_3 2H_2O$ *Hydrated copper silicate*

Characteristics: Colour green, blue, bluish green. Streak greenish white. Hardness 2-4. Spec. Gravity 2.0-2.4. Vitreous lustre, opaque, occasionally weakly translucent. Fracture conchoidal. No cleavage. Crysals (crystal system unknown) microscopically small, usually amorphous aggregates, botryoidal, reniform, stalactitic or crusty. An intergrowth of chrysocolla with turquoise and malachite is known as Eilatstone after the locality where it is found, Eilat in Israel.—**Occurrence:** Botryoidal coatings or cleavage infilling of copper ore deposits. Associated minerals azurite, cuprite, dioptase, malachite.—**Localities:** Found in many of the old mines of Cornwall; also at—Roughton Gill, near Caldbeck, Cumbria; USSR (Urals; Kazakhstan); Chile; USA (Arizona; Nevada); Zaire (Katanga); South West Africa.—**Uses:** Locally worked as an important ore of copper. Beautifully coloured varieties worked as gemstones usually with convex cut, and for objets d'art.—**Illustration:** Chrysocolla aggregate partially overgrown by quartz, Arizona, USA.

Zircon

ZrSiO₄   Zirconium silicate

$ZrSiO_4$ *Zirconium silicate*

Characteristics: Colour yellow, brown, rarely colourless, red, blue or green. Streak white. Hardness 7½. Spec. Gravity 4.6-4.7. Adamantine to vitreous lustre. Transparent to translucent, sometimes nearly opaque. Fracture conchoidal, very brittle. Cleavage imperfect along length of crystals. Crystals (tetragonal system) mainly intergrown, short prisms with pyramidal end faces.—**Occurrence:** Accessory mineral in igneous rocks, crystalline schists and sandstones. Gem quality zircon mainly in alluvial deposits.—**Localities:** France (Haute-Loire); Norway (South east coast); Cambodia; Burma; Thailand; Sri Lanka; Brazil; Madagascar; Australia.—**Uses:** In the production of steels, and in the production of fire and acid resistant materials, such as bricks; transparent zircon is used as a gemstone. The yellow-red to red-brown gem varieties are called hyacinth, and jacinth.—**Illustration:** Zircon crystals on matrix, Urals, USSR.

Olivine
Peridot *(Mg,Fe)₂SiO₄ Magnesium iron silicate*

Characteristics: Colour olive green, yellowish, brownish, rarely grey or colourless. Streak white. Hardness 6½-7. Spec. Gravity 3.2-4.4. Vitreous lustre, appears oily on broken surfaces, transparent to translucent. Fracture conchoidal. Cleavage imperfect, brittle. Well formed crystals (orthorhombic system), very rare, short, stout prisms, striated along their length. aggregates compact, granular, dense, frequently as nodules.—**Occurrence:** In igneous rocks such as basalt and gabbro, often as a major constituent and as monomineralic nodules; in some types of metamorphic rock; and in alluvial deposits.—**Localities:** Mull and Skye, Scotland; Northern Ireland; Norway (Nordfjord); Burma (Magok); USA (Arizona; Hawaii; New Mexico); Zebirget Island, Red Sea.—**Uses:** In the production of fire-resistant bricks. Beautifully coloured, transparent stones worked as gemstones (commercially known as peridot), usually cut to a table and step cuts but also with brilliant cut and as cabochons.—**Illustration:** Olivine aggregate from Tenerife, Canary Islands, and cut peridot from Arizona, USA.

Topaz
Al₂SiO₄(F,OH)₂ Aluminium fluo-silicate

Characteristics: Colour yellow, brown, colourless, blue, red, green. Streak white. Hardness 8. Spec. Gravity 3.5-3.6. Vitreous lustre, transparent to translucent. Fracture subconchoidal to uneven. Cleavage perfect across length of crystals, therefore care needed when cutting. Crystals (orthorhombic system) with striations along their length, prismatic, with richly facetted terminations, commonly of eight-sided cross section. Large crystals weighing many kilogrammes are known. Aggregates compact or bladed.—**Occurrence:** As single crystals in cavities, in pegmatites also in alluvial deposits.—**Localities:** A number of localities in Cornwall; also Lundy Island; Aberdeenshire; and the Mourne Mountains; Brazil; Sri Lanka; Burma; USSR (Urals; Transbaikalia).—**Uses:** For jewellery. Coloured stones with step and other cuts, colourless with diamond cut, varieties with inclusions as cabochons. Amethyst which can be turned yellow by heating is called golden topaz; true topaz is also called gem topaz.—**Illustration:** Topaz crystal in quartz and 53 carat cut topaz, Brazil.

Actinolite
Amphibole group

Ca$_2$(Mg,Fe)$_5$Si$_8$O$_{22}$(OH)$_2$ Complex calcium silicate

Characteristics: Colour green. Streak white. Hardness 5-6. Spec. Gravity 3.0-3.4. Vitreous and silky lustre, transparent to translucent. Fracture splintery, tough. Two good cleavages along the length of crystals intersecting at an angle of 120 degrees. Crystals (monoclinic system) long bladed, acicular or fibrous. Aggregates elongated to radiating. A tough felted variety of actonolite is called nephrite.—**Occurrence:** In talc and chlorite schists, as actinolite schists and disseminated in serpentinite and marble.—**Localities:** Isle of Skye and Durness, Scotland; Switzerland. Nephrite in Germany (Harz; Harzburg); Poland; USSR (Lake Baikal region); New Zealand; Polynesia.—**Uses:** Finely fibrous actinolite mined as asbestos for fire and acid resistant materials. Nephrite in prehistoric times as raw material for weapons and tools, nowadays for jewellery and objets d'art; known as jade in the jewellery trade.—**Illustration:** Elongate actinolite in talc-mica schist, Hohe Tauern, Austria.

Chrysotile
(Serpentine group)

Mg$_3$Si$_2$O$_5$(OH)$_4$ Basic magnesium silicate

Characteristics: Colour pale yellow, pale green to whitish, rarely brown. Streak white. Hardness 2½-4. Spec. Gravity 2.5-2.6. Silky lustre, partially with golden sheen, translucent to opaque. Fracture conchoidal, splintery. Crystals (monoclinic system) small, usually as long, fine fibres. Aggregates dense or as parallel fibres. Fibres up to 16 cm long are known.—**Occurrence:** On joints in serpentinite. —**Localities:** Found in the Liskeard area of Cornwall, and near Ivybridge, Devon; Austria; Cyprus; USSR (Urals); Canada (Quebec); South Africa (Transvaal); Rhodesia.—**Uses:** Finely fibrous aggregates worked for fireproof and alkali resistant asbestos cloth, and as in insulation material. Also used in the building industry for asbestos cement, in the motor industry for brake linings and in the rubber and paper industries as an additive.—**Illustration:** Chrysotile asbestos, Black Lake, Quebec, Canada.

Almandine (Garnet group)

Fe$_3$Al$_2$Si$_3$O$_{12}$ Iron aluminium silicate

Characteristics: Colour dark red with a tint of violet, brown, occasionally black. Streak white. Hardness 6-7½. Spec. Gravity 4.0-4.2. Vitreous to resinous lustre, transparent to translucent. Fracture subconchoidal. Cleavage none. Crystals (cubic system) usually rhombdodecahedra, icositetrahedra, also both forms in combination, rarely cubes or octahedra, intergrown and as distinct crystals. Aggregates compact, dense, granular.—**Occurrence:** Rather common in metamorphic rocks, partially rock forming, and in alluvial deposits. —**Localities:** St Just, Cornwall; Sweden (Falun); Madagascar; Sri Lanka; India; USSR (Urals).—**Uses:** Used for centuries in jewellery. In order to make lighter the deep red colour of almandine, the undersides of stones are occasionally hollowed out on cutting. Employed with a facetted cut or as cabochons. Non-gem quality almandine is used as an abrasive.—**Illustration:** Almandine in mica schist from Zillertal, Austria.

Further varieties in the garnet group are:-

Pyrope
Colour red with a brownish tint. Found at Elie, Fife, Scotland. A rose-red or purplish variety of pyrope is called rhodolite.

Spessartine
Colour orange to red-brown. Formerly found at Spessart, Germany, presently mainly in Sri Lanka, Brazil and the USA.

Grossular
Colour green, yellowish, brownish. A green colour is preferred for jewellery. Found in Devon and Cornwall, and County Donegal, Eire. A yellow to brown-red variety of grossular is called Hesonite.

Andradite
Colour brown-black to deep red, usually not of gem quality. From Devon and Cornwall. A green variety suitable for jewellery is called demantoid, and an opaque black variety melanite.

Uvarovite
Colour emerald-green, sometimes of gem quality.

Staurolite

(Fe,Mg)$_2$ (Al,Fe)$_9$ Si$_4$ O$_{20}$ (O,OH)$_2$
Iron magnesium aluminium silicate

Characteristics: Colour reddish brown to black-brown. Streak white to yellowish. Hardness 7-7½. Spec. Gravity 3.7-3.8. Vitreous to resinous lustre. Translucent to nearly opaque. Fracture subconchodal. One distinct cleavage. Crystals (monoclinic system) short or long prismatic with six-sided cross section, intergrown. Occasionally forms granular aggregates. Frequently as cross-shaped interpenetration twins, the two parts crossing at right angles or 60°.—**Occurrence:** In metamorphic rocks, sometimes concentrated in alluvial deposits. Associated minerals are andulusite, brookite, cordierite, mica, garnet, kyanite, magnetite, quartz.—**Localities:** Norway (Oslo district); Switzerland (Tessin); Czechoslovakia (Mahren); France (Brittany); USA (New Hampshire and Tennessee).—**Uses:** Occasionally worn as costume jewellery; twinned crystals sometimes carried as amulets.—**Illustration:** Single crystal and interpenetration twins, Brittany, France; Virginia, USA; Minas Gerais, Brazil.

Diopside (Pyroxene group)

CaMg Si$_2$O$_6$ Calcium magnesium silicate

Characteristics: Colour green, rarely white, yellow, colourless. Streak white. Hardness 5½-6½. Spec. Gravity 3.3. Vitreous lustre, translucent, to opaque. Fracture uneven. Two good cleavages meet at an angle of 90 degrees. Crystals (monoclinic system) prisms with square or eight-sided cross-sections. Aggregates massive, granular. A compact voilet-blue variety from Piedmont in Italy is called violan.—**Occurrence:** An essential component of certain igneous rocks (particularly gabbro, basalt, and dolerite), in veins and in cavities; in igneous and metamorphic rocks.—**Localities:** Cornwall; County Donegal, Eire; Italy (Vesuvius; Piedmont); Sweden (Wermland); USSR (Urals); USA (California); Burma; India; Madagascar.—**Uses:** The emerald green chrome-diopside for jewellery, either facetted or as cabochons.—**Illustration:** Chrome-diopside group from Outokumpu, Finland.

Jadeite Pyroxene group
NaAl Si$_2$O$_6$ Sodium aluminium silicate

Characteristics: Colour mainly green or white, also nearly black. Streak white. Hardness 6. Spec. Gravity 3.2-3.4. Vitreous lustre, pearly lustre on cleavage surfaces, opaque to translucent. Fracture splintery, extraordinarily tough. Cleavage good parallel to length of crystals. Crystals (monoclinic system) rare and usually small. Aggregates dense, finely fibrous to granular. An iron-rich, green-black variety of jadeite is called chloromelanite.—**Occurrence:** As layers in serpentinites and some other types of metamorphic rocks, and as river pebbles.—**Localities:** Italy (Val di Susa, Piedmont); Burma (Tawmar); China (Eastern Turkistan); Tibet; Guatemala; Japan; Mexico; USA (California).—**Uses:** As material for jewellery, ornaments and cultural objects. Known commercially as jade. The most valuable is imperial jade, an emerald green coloured jadeite which is translucent in thin pieces.—**Illustration:** Jadeite aggregate and cut and polished chloromelanite, Yunnan, China.

Dioptase
CuSiO$_2$ (OH)$_2$ Hydrated copper silicate

Characteristics: Colour emerald green. Streak green to bluish. Hardness 5. Spec. Gravity 3.3. Vitreous lustre, Transparent to translucent. Fracture conchoidal to uneven, brittle. Cleavage perfect. Crystals (trigonal system) rare, small, short columnar, prismatic. Aggregates compact but rare.—**Occurrence:** In the oxidised zones of copper ore deposits on cleavages in limestone, occasionally also in alluvial deposits. Associated minerals are calcite, chrysocolla, hemimorphite, malachite, wulfenite.—**Localities:** USSR (Kirghiz Steppes); Chile (Copiapo); Peru; USA (Arizona); South West Africa; Zaire (Katanga).—**Uses:** Not used as an ore because of its rarity. Cut and polished by collectors for jewellery as facetted stones or cabochons. Formerly mistaken for emerald on acount of its colour.—**Illustration:** Dioptase group from Tsumeb, South West Africa.

Sodalite

$Na_8 Al_6 Si_6 O_{24} Cl_2$ *Sodium aluminium chloro-silicate.*

Characteristics: Colour blue, grey, also yellowish white, reddish, greenish or colourless. streak white. Hardness 5½-6. Spec. Gravity 2.3. Vitreous lustre, transparent to translucent. Fracture uneven to conchoidal. Cleavage poor. Crystals (cubic system) rare and very small, mostly rhomb-dodecahedra, only occasionally cubes or octahedra. Aggregates compact, granular, usually penetrated by veins of white calcite.—**Occurrence:** In silica-poor igneous rocks.—**Localities:** Germany (Eifel); France (Auvergne); Rumania (Siebenburgen); USSR (Urals); Brazil (Bahia); Canada (Ontario); USA. (Maine); South West Africa; India.—**Uses:** For jewellery e.g. rings, pendants, necklaces and as objets d'art.—**Illustration:** Sodalite aggregate cut by white calcite veins, Canada.

Kunzite   (Spodumene group)

$LiAlSi_2 O_5$ *Lithium aluminium silicate.*

Characteristics: Colour pink to light violet. Streak white. Hardness 6½-7. Spec. Gravity 3.0-3.2. Vitreous lustre, weak pearly lustre on cleavage surfaces, transparent. Fracture uneven, splintery. Cleavage perfect along length of crystals. Crystals (monoclinic system) occasionally very large, prismatic and tabular; striated along their length. Aggregates massive or bladed.—**Occurrence:** In lithiump-rich pegmatites. associated minerals are amblygonite, beryl, cassiterite, tourmaline.—**Localities:** Madagascar (Antsirabe); USA (California; Maine); Brazil (Minas Gerais); Burma.—**Uses:** Beautifully coloured varieties cut and polished for jewellery as facetted stones, cabochons or as beads. By reason of the perfect cleavage it is difficult to work. Green varieties are called hiddenite, but it is less widely used as a gemstone than kunzite.—**Illustration:** Kunzite cleavage mass, Brazil.

Benitoite

BaTiSi₃O₉   Barium titanium silicate.

Characteristics: Colour light blue, dark blue, rarely colourless, partially flecked. Streak white. Hardness 6-6½. Bright vitreous lustre, transparent to translucent. Fracture conchoidal, brittle. No cleavage. Crystals (trigonal system), small and very rare, bipyramidal, intergrown. Benitoite does not occur as aggregates.—**Occurrence:** In cavities and veins of metamorphic rocks (glaucophane schists). Associated minerals are anatase, glaucophane, natrolite, neptunite.—**Localities:** Only at Mount Diabolo in San Benito County, California, USA.—**Uses:** Clear and uniformly coloured crystals cut and polished as gemstones.—**Illustration:** Benitoite group from California, USA.

Hemimorphite

Zn₄ Si₂ O₇ (OH)₂ . H₂O   Hydrated basic zinc silicate.

Characteristics: Colour blue, green, brown, colourless, white. Streak white. Hardness 4½-5. Spec. Gravity 3.4-3.5. Vitreous lustre, pearly lustre on cleavage surfaces, transparent to translucent. Fracture conchoidal to uneven. Cleavage perfect. Crystals (orthorhombic system) tabular, columnar, fibrous, sometimes arranged in fan shapes. Aggregates nodular, massive, stalactitic, crusty, mamillated, rarely granular or earthy.—**Occurrence:** In the oxidised zones of lead-zinc sulphide ore deposits. Crystals only in cavities.—**Localities:** Roughton Gill, Cumbria; Wanlockhead, Dumfriesshire; and Matlock, Derbyshire; Italy (Sardinia).—**Uses:** Important ore of zinc. Coloured varieties for jewellery, blue-white banded aggregates worked as objets d'art.—**Illustration:** Fan shaped formation of hemimorphite from Mexico.

Tourmaline

Na(Mg,Fe,Li,Al,Mn)$_3$ Al$_5$ (BO$_3$)$_3$ Si$_6$ O$_{18}$
Complex and variable aluminium boro-silicate.

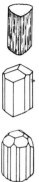

Characteristics: Colour pink, red, yellow, brown, green, blue, violet, colourless, black, multi-coloured. Some tourmalines show different colours in the same crystal, for instance it may have a red core with white and green outer layers, or a green core with an outer red layer. Streak white. Hardness 7. Spec. Gravity 3.0-3.2. Vitreous lustre, transparent to nearly opaque. Fracture uneven to finely conchoidal. Cleavage very poor. Crystals (trigonal system) intergrown or distinct. Mostly elongated, prismatic to acicular, with triangular cross section but curved sides; striations parallel to the length of crystals. Very large crystals known. Aggregates columnar, often several prisms in combination, fibrous, dense, radiating, rarely compact.—**Occurrence:** In granites (in cavities and joints), pegmatites and in alluvial deposits.—**Localities:** Numerous localities in Devon and Cornwall; Switzerland (Tessin); Italy (Elba); Brazil (Minas Gerais; Bahia); Sri Lanka; Madagascar; Mozambique; USSR (Urals; Transbaikalia); USA (California; Maine; Colorado); in addition many countries in Africa and South East Asia.—**Uses:** Much prized gemstone. It has different names according to colour: achroite (colourless), rubellite (pink to red), dravite (yellow to brown), indicolite (blue), schorl (black). Colourless tourmaline is rare. The most prized are pink and emerald coloured stones. The Dutch who, at the beginning of the 18th century, introduced tourmaline from Ceylon to Europe, used this mineral among others to clean their meerschaum pipes. They took advantage thereby of a particular quality of tourmaline. If it is heated and then, when cooled, it is pressed or rubbed, it becomes electrically charged and then attracts dust, particles, ash and small scraps of paper. The Dutch, for this reason, call tourmaline 'Aschentrekker' or ash attractor.—**Illustration:** Tourmaline group, California, USA (about ¾ natural size).

Coral

Calcium carbonate + magnesia + organic material.

Characteristics: Colour red, pink, white, often flecked white and soft pink, very rarely also blue and black. Streak white. Hardness 3-4. Spec. Gravity 2.6-2.7. Naturally dull, when polished has a vitreous lustre, opaque. Fracture irregular, splintery. No cleavage. Coral is a mixture and, therefore strictly speaking a rock.—**Occurrence:** As reefs and single colonies. Only colony-forming corals are used in the jewellery trade. They are formed of small polyps which secrete calcareous material. Sensitive to heat, acids and washing in hot water.—**Localities:** Corals only grow in warm tropical seas particularly the Caribbean, the west and central Pacific, and off the Coast of East Africa.—**Uses:** For necklaces, rings, brooches and for objets d'art. The most coveted is the precious coral of uniform ox-blood colour.—**Illustration:** Precious coral from Sicily.

Amber

About $C_{10}H_{16}O$ A mixture of different resins.

Characteristics: Colour light yellow to brown, red, whitish, rarely also blue, black, greenish. Streak white. Hardness 2-2½. Spec. Gravity 1.0-1.3. Greasy lustre, transparent to opaque. Fracture conchoidal, brittle. No cleavage, only amorphous aggregates, nodular or drop-shaped, reniform, sometimes covered by an earthy weathered crust.—**Occurrence:** In some geologically recent sedimentary rocks, and as beach pebbles. Amber is of organic origin, being the hardened resin of pine trees. strictly speaking amber is not a mineral.—**Localities:** Palmnikken in East Prussia; countries bordering the Baltic Sea; Sicily; Rumania; Burma; Canada; USA (Atlantic area).—**Uses:** Since prehistoric times for jewellery and cultural objects, nowadays also for technical purposes. Small fragments made into pressed amber under high pressures.—**Illustration:** Amber with carbonaceous inclusions and insects, East Prussia.

Igneous Rocks—plutonic

Granite

Characteristics: Colour grey, yellowish, bluish, reddish to red, rarely greenish. The general impression of colour is given by the feldspar. Despite containing different minerals and having different colours granite always appears light when freshly broken. Cut and polished surfaces have a darker appearance. The commonest minerals of granite are plagioclase feldspar, orthoclase feldspar and quartz. Dark mica (biotite) and/or light mica (muscovite) are commonly present in small amounts. In rare varieties a range of other minerals may be present in significant amounts. Quartz usually appears glassy, and the feldspar may be pink or white. Coarse-grained texture. Individual crystals may vary in size, but can usually be recognised with the naked eye. Feldspar often develops good crystal outlines. In granite there is usually no visibly recognisable preferred orientation of the minerals in the rock. Granite is generally compact but small cavities, with good crystals in them, sometimes occur.—**Origin:** As a result of very slow cooling of molten rock material, called magma, in the depths of the Earth's crust. On later erosion of the covering rocks, granite may eventually be exposed at the surface. Though many granites are very old, they are not restricted to any particular geological period: there are granites of all geological ages.—**Localities:** Varieties of granite are the most common plutonic igneous rocks. They occur in Devon and Cornwall; north Wales; the Lake District; the Cheviots; the Southern Uplands of Scotland; and at many places in the Scottish Highlands. Granite is quarried in Germany; Finland; France (Auvergne; Brittany); Italy (Piedmont); Norway; Scotland; Sweden; Spain (Pyrenees); USSR.; and also in many parts of the rest of the world.—**Uses:** See page 114.—**Illustration:** Above: Gefrees granite, rough broken surface, Fichtelgebirge, Germany. The surface appears uniformly light, the individual minerals easily recognised. Below: Waldstein granite, polished, Fichtelgebirge, Germany. The polished surface of the granite appears darker than the broken surface and the individual minerals are even more clearly differentiated.

Granite

Uses: Granite is a well known building and construction stone. It has a high abrasion hardness, is very resistant to weathering and extremely resistant to chemical attack. Because of the high feldspar content it can be worked easily but implements cutting granite wear out relatively quickly owing to the high quartz content.

Grey varieties are used principally as kerb and paving stones, as road metal and ballast. Coloured granites are favoured for facades, wall cladding, flooring, fountains and sculptures.

The geologist names granites mainly according to their constituent minerals, but occasionally according to some outstanding texture or structure, for instance alkali granite, augite granite, biotite-, hornblende-, muscovite-, two-mica granite, or graphic granite. In southern Finland the so-called rapakivi granites contain large, round yellow or red feldspars (orthoclase) which are mantled by lighter coloured feldspar (oligoclase). If the rim is not as resistant to weathering as the core, the use of rapakivi granite is greatly limited. The architect and stone mason distinguish between granites on the basis of colour and locality or origin, e.g. Peterhead granite (quarried near Aberdeen and used all over Britain), and Shap granite (quarried at Shap, Cumbria, and used, mostly decoratively, on many public buildings. It is easily distinguished by the large, pink, rectangular feldspars). Also Arno granite (Thüringia, East Germany); Baveno rosso (Italy); Cornish granite, Geretelbach granite (Black Forest, Germany); Gotenrot granite (Sweden); Granite bleu (France); Korall granite (USSR); Weingraben granite (Austria). Rocks which mineralogically are not granites are occasionally known as such commercially e.g. *Belgian granite* (Petit granite), the trade name for a dark grey to black bituminous limestone with some white spots. The rock is actually a carbonaceous limestone. Granitmarmor (Granite marble) is the trade name for a limestone from southern Germany: It is neither granite nor marble.—**Illustration:** Upper left: Kosseine granite, polished, Fichtelgebirge, Germany. Upper right: Epprechtstein granite, polished, Fichtelgebirge Germany. Below: Gotenrot granite, polished, Sweden.

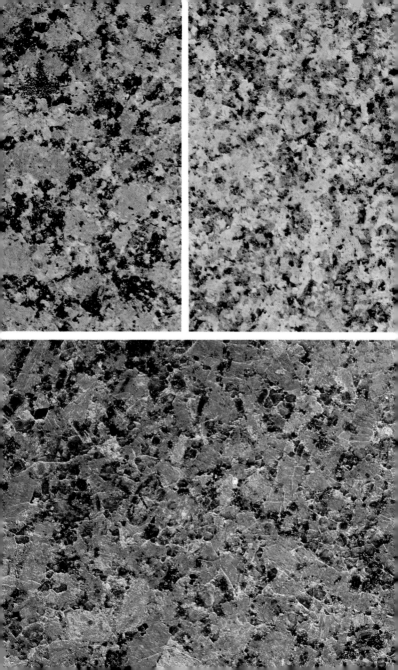

Syenite   (Illustration upper left)

Characteristics: Colour grey, reddish, bluish. Generally a light appearance. Essential orthoclase and/or sodium-rich plagioclase feldspar; biotite, or hornblende also commonly occur. Quartz may be present in small amounts. Minerals generally recognisable with the naked eye, and of no preferred orientation.—**Origin:** By crystallisation of magma deep in the Earth's crust.—**Localities:** Ben Loyal, near Tongue, Sutherland, and the area near Ledmore, east of Ullapool, Ross and Cromarty, Scotland; Norway; Sweden.—**Uses:** Building stone.—**Illustration:** Syenite, upper Italy.

Diorite   (Illustration upper right)

Characteristics: Colour grey-white. Essential plagioclase; hornblende and/or biotite invariably present. Quartz may be present in small amounts. Minerals usually recognisable with the naked eye, and they may or may not have a preferred orientation.—**Origin:** From molten magma deep in the Earth's crust.—**Localities:** Found at a number of places in the Scottish Highlands, the Channel Islands, and elsewhere.—**Uses:** Building stone.—**Illustration:** Diorite, lower Austria.

Gabbro   (Illustration lower left)

Characteristics: Colour dark green, greenish, black when polished. Essential plagioclase and augite; olivine commonly present. Individual minerals can usually be recognised with the naked eye.—**Origin:** From molten magma in the depths of the Earth's crust.—**Localities:** N.E. Scotland; the islands of Skye and Mull; Carrock Fell; Cumbria; the Channel Islands.—**Uses:** Building stone, monuments, gravestones.—**Illustration:** Gabbro, Odenwald, Germany.

Peridotite   (Illustration lower right)

Characteristics: Colour dark grey, green-black. Essential olivine and augite.—**Origin:** From magma crystallized deep in the Earth's crust.—**Localities:** The Lizard area, Cornwall. —**Uses:** Green varieties as decorative stone.—**Illustration:** Harzburgite, a variety of peridotite, Harz, Germany.

Orbicular diorite

Characteristics: Colour whitish grey. Generally light appearance, polished surfaces appear darker owing to the grey-black tones of component minerals. Essential minerals are plagioclase feldspar and hornblende; biotite and quartz are also often present. Orthoclase feldspar may occur in small amounts. Owing to the ordered arrangement of the minerals it shows a structure with concentrically arranged spheres (orbicular structure) in a groundmass with a normal, granular texture.—**Origin:** Crystallization of a magma; but the way in which the orbicular structure is produced is still not fully understood.—**Localities:** Alderney in the Channel Islands; Corsica; Finland; Peru.—**Uses:** As a monumental stone and decorative stone and for objets d'art.—**Illustration:** Cut and polished orbicular diorite, and cabochon, Corsica.

Larvikite

Characteristics: Colour light or dark blue-grey, multicoloured, pearly schiller. Essential minerals are orthoclase and augite. Quartz is present but only in small amounts. Minerals are distinguishable with the naked eye; they are inter-locking and show no preferred orientation.—**Origin:** By the slow cooling of molten rock material deep in the Earth's crust. Larvikite belongs to the syenite family.—**Localities:** Southern Norway, light varieties from Tvedal, dark from Klåstad.—**Uses:** Architectural stone, principally for facades, sometimes for gravestones. Very common as a facing stone on shops, banks, and other buildings. Because of the schiller, which resembles that of labradorite, larvikite is sometimes so called commercially. On the basis of general appearance the building trade distinguishes the light varieties (blue pearl) from the dark (emerald pearl).—**Illustration:** Below left: polished emerald pearl. Below right: polished blue pearl, Norway.

Igneous Rocks—volcanic (extrusive)

Pumice

Characteristics: Colour grey, yellowish, whitish, reddish; the general impression is usually light. Not crystalline, a glassy rock. The specific gravity of the actual rock material is 2.4, the density of the rock mass, by reason of numerous pores is, however, less than 1 so that pumice floats on water. Frequently pumice appears very much like foam.—**Origin:** By the rapid cooling of a gas-rich lava on the Earth's surface.—**Localities:** Germany (Eifel); Italy (Lipari Islands and elsewhere); Iceland.—**Uses:** In the building industry in the production of light weight building materials. As an abrasive, and as 'pumice stone' for cleaning the hands. The numerous pores mean that the surface of pumice remains continually rough. In industry natural pumice is replaced by a pumice produced artifically from quartz sand and emery.—**Illustration:** Pumice, Lipari Island, Italy.

Obsidian

Characteristics: Colour dark grey to black, brown, greenish. Rock masses not crystallised but formed of natural glass. Very compact and hard, dark grey translucent at the edges. It has a characteristic conchoidal and sharp-edged fracture.—**Origin:** By very rapid cooling of lava at the surface of the Earth and in small intrusions. Obsidians which contain a few crystals are called pitchstone.—**Localities:** Italy; Greece; Iceland; Mexico.—**Uses:** Used in the Stone Age for weapons and implements because its sharp-edged fracture meant it could be made into cutting tools, arrow heads etc. Presently sometimes worked for objets d'art and costume jewellery.—**Illustration:** Obsidian with typical conchoidal fracture, Lipari Island, Italy.

Basalt

Characteristics: Colour dark grey, grey-black, black. Essential minerals present are plagioclase and augite. Olivine may be present. There are many varieties of basalt with slightly different mineral compositions. Fine-grained and may contain small rounded cavities, called vesicles, which were formed as gas bubbles when the rock was molten.—**Origin:** By cooling of molten lava at or near the Earth's surface.—**Localities:** The most abundant of the volcanic igneous rocks. Found in Northern Ireland; Skye; Mull; Staffa etc., Scotland.—**Uses:** As road metal and ballast.—**Illustration:** Basalt, Rhineland, Germany.

Amygdaloidal basalt   (Illustration top right)

Characteristics: Colour darky-grey to black. Essential minerals present are plagioclase and augite. These rocks are varieties of basalt. Fine-grained texture. They are characterised by numerous round or almond-shaped masses of minerals (agate, calcite, chlorite, quartz etc., and these are called amygdales).—**Origin:** The amygdales form by the crystallization of minerals in gas cavities (vesicles) in lava.—**Localities:** Various places in the Midland valley of Scotland, and in the Western Isles such as Mull and Skye.—**Uses:** As road metal. Well formed minerals occur occasionally in the amygdales and cavities.—**Illustration:** Amygdaloidal basalt, Hunsrück, Rheinland-Pfalz, Germany.

Diabase   (Illustration below)

Characteristics: Colour grey-green, black-green. The essential minerals are plagioclase and augite; olivine, serpentine, and chlorite also occur. Diabase belongs to the basalt group. Texture medium-grained, and homogeneous.—**Origin:** Essentially the same composition as basalt. The name diabase was formerly used, and in some places is still used, to signify a rock of basaltic composition which had been altered. Usually occurs in small intrusions (dykes).—**Localities:** Germany (Harz; Fichtelgibirge); southern Sweden.—**Uses:** As road metal or railway ballast, coloured varieties as architectural stone. Numerous trade names.—**Illustration:** Polished diabase, France.

Sedimentary Rocks

Conglomerate

Characteristics: Colour grey, yellowish, reddish. Different minerals are present because the rock consists of pebbles in a matrix of sand. The pebbles are commonly of limestone, quartzite, granite, or gneiss. Interstices may be filled with sand or clay. When cemented can be an extremely tough rock.—**Origin:** By the consolidation of boulder and pebble deposits. Usually formed close to the edge of the sea where such deposits are common.—**Localities:** Many places. In various parts of Hertfordshire a well known conglomerate, known as 'Hertfordshire Puddingstone', is to be found. —**Uses:** As rough hewn blocks for monuments, fountains, and for landscaping gardens, as sawn slabs for facades. In commerce and the stone industry there is no clear distinction between conglomerate and breccia.—**Illustration:** Cut and polished conglomerate, Brannenburg, Bavaria, Germany.

Breccia

Characteristics: Colour grey, reddish, variously coloured. Different minerals are present because, like conglomerate, breccia consists of fragments of any type of rock in a finer-grained matrix. The fragments must be angular, in contrast to the rounded pebbles or boulders of conglomerates. The rocks comprising the fragments may be sedimentary, metamorphic or igneous in origin. They may be large or small, all about the same size, or variable in size.—**Origin:** As a result of cementing together of angular rock fragments with finer-grained sediment, usually sand or mud. The original unconsolidated material was usually a scree deposit probably heaped against a cliff.—**Localities:** Various localities, but usually only in relatively small amounts.—**Uses:** As a cladding for facades, brightly coloured varieties as decorative stones. Limestone breccias which are compact and easily cut are often known commercially as marble. Often no clear distinction is made between breccia and conglomerate.—**Illustration:** Cut and polished limestone breccia, France.

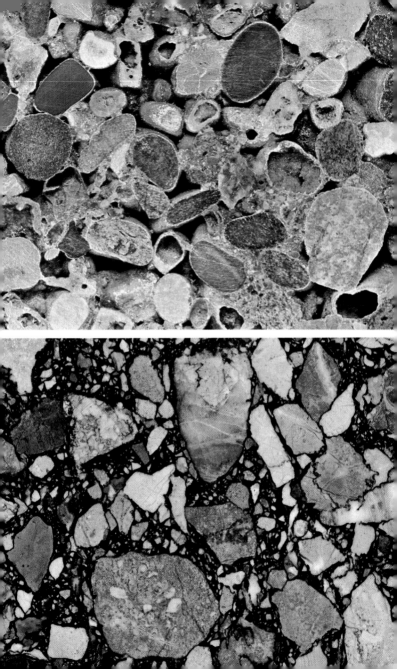

Sandstone

Characteristics: Colour grey, brown yellow or red, but other colours also found. The minerals present in most sandstones are mainly quartz, feldspar and mica. Quartz-rich varieties cemented by silica are called quartzite, coarse-grained varieties rich in feldspar are called arkose. Rock fabric loose to hard and compact; the pore spaces between the sand grains may constitute 25% or more of the volume of the rock. The size of individual grains varies between 0.06 and 2 mm in diameter. The grains may be rounded, or sharply angular. Most sandstones are water-laid and show distinct layering (bedding).—**Origin:** By the cementation of sand grains with argillaceous, calcareous or siliceous material frequently mixed with particles of other minerals. Many sandstone names derive from such additions, for instance ferruginous or calcareous sandstone. Sandstones are represented among rocks of all geological periods.—**Localities:** Sandstone is the most widely distributed of all sedimentary rocks, and is found in all parts of the British Isles. Red sandstones of Triassic age are widespread in the north-west Midlands, Cheshire and Lanchashire. Greensand occurs in south-east England, and red Torridonian sandstones and white quartzites are widespread in the north-west of Scotland.—**Uses:** Fine-grained and quartz-rich varieties for monumental stones and facades, less hard kinds for sculpture, very compact and quartz-rich varieties for flooring and as broken rock for road metal and railway ballast. In the middle ages sandstone was the most favoured material for building castles, and the huge Anglican Cathedral in Liverpool is of a red Triassic sandstone. In the last decades the use of sandstone has increased considerably, but many varieties, by reason of their calcareous cement, are attacked and crumble as a result of attack by gases in smoke in the air.—**Illustration:** Above: Sandstone (Porta Sandstone), rough broken, Westphalia, Germany. Below left: Sandstone (Main sandstone) cut surface, Unterfranken. Below right: Sandstone (Buntsandstein) with axed surface, Black Forest, Germany.

Calcareous tufa

Characteristics: Colour yellow to brown, white, reddish. Calcite is virtually the only mineral present. Calcareous tufa is a type of limestone. The overall density is rather low owing to the spongy structure with large pores; layering rarely apparent. Compact varieties are called travertine.—**Origin:** By crystallisation of calcium carbonate around springs and in caves, but rarely very extensive. Some deposits, particularly those associated with hot springs, have the form of terraces or cascades.—**Localities:** Central Italy; Turkey (Hierapolis). —**Uses:** As a lightweight building stone.—**Illustration:** Calcareous tufa, broken surface, Upper Bavaria, Germany.

Travertine

Characteristics: Colour yellow to brown, white to grey. Calcite is virtually the only mineral present. Travertine is a type of limestone. Although containing many cavities, it is very compact and easily cut. May be strongly or faintly bedded which on a cut surface has a very decorative appearance.—**Origin:** By deposition of calcium carbonate at springs, probably partly through the agency of plants and bacteria. Deposits frequently have the form of terraces or cascades but are rarely very extensive.—**Localities:** Italy (Sabine Hills; Tuscany; Sicily); Hungary; Rumania; Yugoslavia; Turkey.—**Uses:** For facades and floors. Numerous trade names. Travertine weathers readily in the corrosive atmosphere of towns. Therefore it is replaced for garden and paving slabs by more resistant artificial stones.—**Illustration:** Cut Roman Travertine, Italy.

Limestone   (Illustration above left, below left and right)

Characteristics: Colour usually white to grey but all other tones also possible in consequence of the presence of impurities. Calcite is virtually the only mineral present. There is, however, a transition to dolomite. Most limestones are bedded and contain fossils.—**Origin:** Formed on the sea bed from the accumulated remains of the skeletons and shells of dead organisms; also from the precipitation of calcium carbonate directly from sea water.—**Localities:** In many places e.g. Derbyshire and other parts of the Pennines; the south of England including the Chalk cliffs of Dover.—**Uses:** In the building industry as a building stone and for facades, for the manufacture of mortar and cement, as a flux in the smelting of iron ore, as a fertiliser. Every hard limestone capable of taking a polish is known in the building industry as marble, although it is not a true marble (see page 134); there are numerous trade names. Limestones in towns undergo intensive weathering because of corrosive gases in the atmosphere.—**Illustration:** Above left: Limestone (Chalky limestone) Champagne, France. Below left. Crinoidal Limestone, Württemberg. Germany. Below right: Coralline limestone, Eifel, Germany.

Dolomite   (Illustration above right)

Characteristics: Colour usually white to grey but all other tones possible as a consequence of the presence of impurities. Dolomite may be virtually the only mineral present, or there may be a transition to a calcite limestone. Rarely well-bedded, contains few fossils. Very similar in appearance to limestone.—**Origin:** By the transformation of limestone as a consequence of the addition of magnesium.—**Localities:** Northumberland, Durham, and Yorkshire. Also the Midland Valley of Scotland.—**Uses:** In the building industry as a building stone and for facades, in the production of mortar, as a blast furnace lining, and for the extraction of magnesium. Dolomite is more resistant to weathering than limestone. Numerous trade names.—**Illustration:** Above right: Dolomite, Fichtelgebirge, Germany.

Flint

Characteristics: Colour usually black with a white crust. A variety of chalcedony. Flint is very fine-grained. It occurs as single nodules, and sometimes in thick sheets parallel to the bedding of the enclosing rocks. Characteristic conchoidal sharp-edged fracture.—**Origin:** From silica gel which probably comes from the skeletons of siliceous animals and plants. The gel collects on the bottom of the sea and eventually hardens and becomes trapped in the accumulating sediment.—**Localities:** Primarily in the chalk in the south and east of England. Also in glacial and river deposits derived from the Chalk.—**Uses:** By reason of its sharp-edged fracture and hardness, used in the stone age for weapons and tools; used to produce sparks when firearms were developed. Presently used as an abrasive and polishing material and also as a mill-stone in ball mills in the cement industry.—**Illustration:** Flint with typical white and porous crust.

Solenhofen Limestone

Characteristics: Colour yellowish to brown. Calcite virtually the only mineral present. Clearly bedded, very uniformly fine-grained.—**Origin:** From the accumulation of the skeletons and shells of dead marine animals on the sea floor, possibly aided by the physical precipitation of calcium carbonate from the water. The fern-like ornament on the bedding planes—the so-called dendrites—are iron-manganese deposits and not fossils. They have nothing to do with living things and are similar to feathery dendritic ice crystals which form on windows in winter.—**Localities:** This is one example of the many kinds of named limestones. Between Solenhofen and Eichstaff in the Frankischen Alb, Germany. There are many fossils in the limestone and it was in this rock that the earliest fossil bird (Archaeopteryx) was found.—**Uses:** As flooring slabs, as wall cladding and for garden landscaping. Because of the uniform grain-size it was formerly used in lithographic printing, and so was known as lithographic limestone.—**Illustration:** Solenhofen Limestone with dendrites, Mittelfranken, Germany.

Metamorphic Rocks

Marble

Characteristics: A wide variety of colours, often unevenly distributed, flecked, streaked and veined. Calcite is virtually the only mineral present. Occasionally, marbles are produced from dolomites and accordingly they carry dolomite. Marble is very compact.—**Origin:** Through the recrystallisation of limestone in the Earth's crust. By this means small crystals grow to form larger ones and the marble acquires its typical sugary texture and translucent appearance which is clearly seen at thin edges. Most of the fossils which may have been present in the original limestone are destroyed. The causes of the change (called metamorphism) are high temperatures caused either by the proximity of igneous intrusions or by deep burial in the Earth's crust, perhaps during the movements which cause the building of mountain ranges.—**Localities:** Because many marble deposits are strongly cleaved, it is often impossible to work them economically. In earlier times white marbles from Greece were the most important, today Carrara Marble from Tuscany, Italy has taken its place. There are smaller occurrences in many parts of Europe including Germany; Sicily; Spain; France; Belgium; and Norway. Very little true marble occurs in Britain. There are localities in Skye and the north-west of Scotland, and a patchy green marble used to be quarried in Connemara, Eire. In commerce and in the stone industry marble has a much wider meaning that in the scientific world. All limestones which are sufficiently compact to take a polish are known commercially as marble, regardless of whether or not they are recrystallised. Even non-calcareous rocks are sometimes called marble if they have a coloured flecked apperance which resembles marble. It is difficult to make a strict distinction between limestone and true marble (crystalline marble) because there may be all stages of transition between the two. For the trade descriptions, see page 136.—**Uses:** Rough-hewn blocks for construction of monuments, cut for facades, wall cladding, steps and floors. Also as a decorative stone for objets d'art and statuettes. Marble quickly corrodes and becomes dull in the fume-laden atmosphere of towns.—**Illustration:** Above left: Polished Carrara marble, Tuscany, Italy. Above right: Polished marble, German red, Oberfranken, Bavaria Germany. Below: Polished marble, Wallenfels, Oberfranken, Bavaria, Germany.

Marble   Trade descriptions

The following are some of the British and Irish rocks known in commerce and industry as marble, although the majority are limestones and not true marbles. Although all of those listed have been used in building and for decorative purposes, few of them are being worked today.

'Purbeck Marble': a freshwater shelly limestone composed essentially of fossil snails, from Swanage, Dorset.

'Tiree Marble': a pink rock with black flecks, from Tiree, Scotland.

'Derby Fossil Marble': A grey and white Carboniferous limestone rich in crinoids, from Derbyshire.

'Frosterly Marble': A Carboniferous limestone rich in corals from Stanhope, Weardale, County Durham.

'Petworth' or *'Sussex Marble':* a shelly Wealden limestone from Petworth, Sussex.

'Dent Marble': a black Carboniferous limestone, from Dent, Yorkshire.

'Onyx Marble: a banded stalagmitic limestone, from Derbyshire.

'Rosewood Marble': a dark brown to black, finely banded Carboniferous limestone from Chatsworth, Derbyshire.

'Birdseye Marble': a very dark crinoidal Carboniferous limestone, from Hopton Wood, Wirksworthe, Derbyshire.

'Duke's Red Marble': a deep red limestone from the Alport Mine, Castleton, Derbyshire.

'Irish Dove': a limestone in shades of grey and white from Eire. *'Galway Black':* a black limestone from Galway, Eire.

Illustration: Above left: Muschelkalk Blaubank, polished, Bavaria, Germany. Above right: Polished Untersberg, Salzburg, Austria.

Serpentinite

Characteristics: Colour various shades of green, often with flecks and patches of black, white or red. The principal mineral is serpentine, with augite, garnet, calcite, hornblende, olivine and talc often present in smaller amounts. Fabric usually massive, but may be layered.—**Origin:** By the alteration of igneous rocks containing abundant olivine (peridotites).—**Localities:** Found over a large part of the Lizard Peninsula, Cornwall; also central Switzerland; Italy (Aosta; Florence; Liguria).—**Uses:** As a decorative stone, and for carving objects. Numerous trade names.—**Illustration:** Serpentine containing white calcite (Verde Alps), Aosta, Italy.

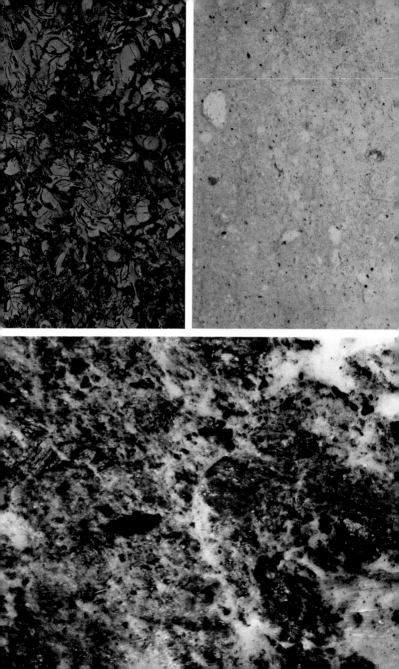

Mica Schist   (Illustration above left)

Characteristics: Colour silver-grey, light brown. Minerals present are mainly quartz and mica (biotite and/or muscovite); feldspar, garnet, kyanite, staurolite. Other minerals may occur. Fabric coarse-grained and distinctly foliated (known as the 'schistosity').—**Origin:** By recrystallization of mudstones and siltstones as a result of high temperatures and pressures deep in the Earth's crust.—**Localities:** Many parts of the Highlands of Scotland; also Anglesey, and parts of Devon.—**Uses:** Architectural stone for cladding. Locally for ballast.—**Illustration:** Mica schist, central Switzerland.

Slate   (Illustration above right)

Characteristics: Colour bluish, greenish to black. Minerals present are mainly micas, but also feldspar, quartz, and chlorite. Fabric dense and strongly foliated so that it splits easily into thin slabs.—**Origin:** By recrystallisation of mudstone and shale as a result of high pressures in the earth's crust.—**Localities:** North Wales and the Lake District.—**Uses:** Roofing slate, facing stone for houses, for the base of billiard tables, and as mountings for electrical switch gear.—**Illustration:** Slate, Tyrol, Austria.

Gneiss   (Illustration below)

Characteristics: Colour variable as forms contrasting dark and light layers. Minerals present are mainly quartz and feldspar, also biotite. Fabric coarse-grained and distinctly layered.—**Origin:** Gneisses are formed mainly in the central part of belts of metamorphic rocks where very high temperatures and pressures occurred, so the rocks recrystallized on a large scale. They are often associated with granites and many gneisses appear to have been near to melting.—**Localities:** Highlands of Scotland, particularly in the north-west.—**Uses:** For monuments, as wall cladding, flooring, as road metal and railway ballast.—**Illustration:** Granite-gneiss, Fichtelgebirge, Germany.

Meteorites

Iron Meteorites

Characteristics: Colour red-brown to black on the outside, steel-bright when cut. Predominantly iron, very rich in nickel. A lamellar structure called Widmanstätten-structure becomes apparent on etching many iron meteorites with nitric acid.—**Origin:** Iron meteorites come from space, and it is postulated that they once formed the core of a planet like our own. Probably about 50 iron meteorites fall on the surface of the Earth each year, though only a few of these are found.—**Localities:** In all continents.—**Uses:** Of no economic importance owing to their rarity.—**Illustration:** Above left: Cut iron Meteorite, Arizona, USA. Above right: Iron Meteorite with Widmanstätten-structure, South West Africa.

Stony Meteorites

Characteristics: External colour jet black, inside brown to dark grey. (This is a fusion crust as the exterior of the meteorite melts on passage through the Earth's atmosphere). Minerals present mainly olivine and augite. Also plagioclase, diopside, magnetite, etc. Fabric is granular or dense, brecciated or glassy.—**Origin:** Stony meteorites come from space, their origin is unknown. They are more common than iron meteorites.—**Localities:** In all continents. Difficult to recognise because of their similarity to terrestrial rocks.—**Uses:** No economic importance.—**Illustration:** Stony meteorite, Mocs, Rumania.

Tektites

Characteristics: Colour black, green, brown. Comprise a silica-rich glass. Some are smooth and shiny, others rough and abraded. Commonly button-shaped.—**Origin:** Tektites are probably formed by the melting of rocks when large meteorites strike the Earth. The molten rock is thrown into the air and freezes rapidly to glassy droplets.—**Localities:** Found only in Australia, parts of south-east Asia, Czechoslovakia, the Ivory coast, and Georgia and Texas in the United States.—**Uses:** Bottle-green varieties, such as are found in Czechoslovakia, cut formerly as jewellery.—**Illustration:** Below left: Green tektite (moldavite), southern Bohemia, Czechoslovakia. Below middle and right: Black tektites, Thailand.

INDEX

*Colour illustration facing text

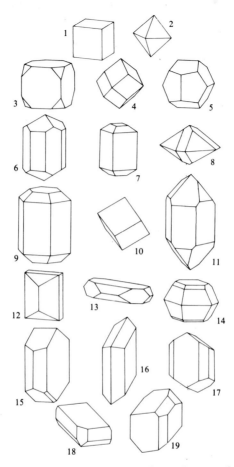

**Drawings of a range of crystals and crystal forms
illustrating the crystal systems**

1 Cube
2 Octahedron
3 Combined cube and octahedron
4 Rhombdodecahedron
5 Pyritohedron
6 A zircon crystal
7 A rutile crystal
8 A cassiterite crystal
9 An apatite crystal
10 Rhombohedron

11 A quartz crystal
12 A staurolite crystal
13 A tabular crystal of baryte
14 A sulphur crystal
15 An orthoclase crystal
16 A gypsum crystal
17 An augite crystal
18 A tabular crystal of rhodonite
19 An axinite crystal